Life in the Galloping Lane

By Karen & David O'Connor

with Nancy Jaffer

PRIMEDIA Equine Network

LIFE IN THE GALLOPING LANE

By Karen & David O'Connor with Nancy Jaffer

Printed in the USA.

First Published in 2004 by PRIMEDIA Equine Network
656 Quince Orchard Road, #600
Gaithersburg, MD 20878
301-977-3900

VP, Group Publishing Director: Susan Harding
Director, Product Marketing: Julie Beaulieu
Editorial Director: Cathy Laws
Copy Editor: Deborah Lyons

**Order by calling 800-952-5813 or
online at www.TheEquineCollection.com**

Book Design: Lauryl Suire Eddlemon
Cover photos: Brant Gamma, www.brantgamma.com
*(Special thanks to Brant, many of whose photos of
the O'Connors over the years appear in these pages.)*

Library of Congress Cataloging-in-Publication Data

O'Connor, Karen, 1958-
Life in the galloping lane : eventing with olympians / Karen & David O'Connor,
with Nancy Jaffer.
p. cm.
ISBN 1-929164-24-6 (hardcover)
1. Eventing (Horsemanship)--United States. 2. O'Connor, Karen, 1958- 3. O'Connor,
David, 1962- 4. Horsemen and horsewomen--United States. 5. Olympics. I. O'Connor,
David, 1962- II. Jaffer, Nancy. III. Title.

SF295.7.O359 2004
798.2'4--dc22

2004016571

To the members of the O'Connor
Event Team, who have a special place
in our hearts, even if they are not
mentioned in these pages.
But most of all, we dedicate this book
to the horses we have ridden:
The famous, the infamous and the
rest, who taught us horsemanship.

—Karen and David

Contents

I wish to acknowledge my husband, Lawrence Nagy, who makes everything possible, and Cathy Laws, as good a friend as she is an editor

—Nancy Jaffer

Foreword

KAREN AND DAVID O'CONNOR spend their lives in perpetual motion, whether they're competing in the biggest equestrian events in the world or seeing to the properties they supervise in a bucolic corner of Virginia's fox-hunting country, halfway between Middleburg and The Plains. These two riders are mates in the truest sense: soulmates, helpmates, and Olympic eventing teammates.

Their home, aptly called "The Haven," doesn't see much of them—but when they manage to spend time there, it offers the refuge for which it is named. Like them, it's handsome and low-key, comfortable, and not ostentatious in the least. Trophies and silver-framed photos of triumphs from England's Badminton and Maryland's Fair Hill to the Olympics and World Championships share shelf space with the books (by an eclectic range of authors, from Dick Francis to David McCullough) that satisfy David's voracious appetite for reading.

In the dining room, where family and friends spend many a convivial evening enjoying Karen's cooking, the couple's Olympic medals hang from their ribbons on pegs, rather than behind glass. That's so visiting Pony Clubbers can have the thrill of trying them on, dreaming about the moment when they, too, may ride in the greatest Games of all.

On a typical day at home, with their enthusiastic terriers and one black Labrador at their heels, Karen and David are busy teaching. (Several students have even bought property in the O'Connors' neck of the woods to be close to them.) Riding something, whether horses or tractors, is, of course, a big part of their schedule, but there's much else to do as well. Going from one stable to the next, they'll be checking horses' legs, supervising staff, and answering (at least sometimes) their constantly ringing cell phones while seeing to the endless details involved in running their business and the farm's.

"We help manage an estate; we don't own an estate," David always points out, lest people mistake him and his wife for independently wealthy land barons, rather than hard workers who have found a way to make their passion for horses pay. It's a task that consumes them all day, nearly every day of the week. The only real down-time the O'Connors have is driving to and from competitions, when they get a chance to think and discuss ideas, programs, or mounts.

Their sport, formerly called "three-day" eventing, requires a lot of planning and preparation. Its three phases derive from an old cavalry exercise that tested both the endurance and the obedience of an officer's charger.

The dressage phase, calling for precision riding, takes place in a compact, white-fenced ring. The movements are similar to the type of maneuvering army mounts had to do on the parade grounds.

The second phase, the heart of eventing, involves cross-country riding at speed in the wide open spaces. That setting may contrast with the confined dressage venue, but to leap down a steep bank, splash through a lake, or clear a yawning ditch also requires control. The original motivation for this test was to prove that a horse and rider could successfully get a vital message through the lines and past obstacles during wartime. Stringent standards and attention to equine welfare have made it a far safer experience for everyone involved than it was for cavalrymen or the sport's pioneers. In war, horses were expendable. But today's riders are not going into battle; there's always another day for them to compete. So they are very conscious of the fact that the horse's quality of life must be a paramount consideration in what they do.

The last phase, stadium jumping, determines who gets to take home the trophy. Held in an arena, it involves far lighter jumps than the solid cross-country obstacles. Poles come down at the merest touch of a hoof, accumulating faults for those unlucky enough to topple a rail.

Bringing a horse through all these exercises in excellent condition (there are strict veterinary checks) and with the willingness to "jump clean" at the end of a strenuous competition is the real test of a horseman or horsewoman. And those two words, "horseman" and "horsewoman," define what David and Karen are at their essence.

That essence also includes wanting to help their sport. So wherever they are, it's likely they'll be involved in something connected to their work for the US Equestrian Federation, of which David became the first president and where Karen serves on the board, or the US Eventing Association, where Karen is active in committee work. These are people who believe in giving back to the horse world that has given them so much. They know it's what you do after you win that counts most.

"We're famous in a very small world," says David, a comment that emphasizes his realistic understanding of what he and his wife have achieved, and of eventing's place in the larger universe. The couple spend much of their time on their own discipline, of course, but they are also interested in helping and learning from other types of horse sports: a breadth of interest that is rather unusual in the very specialized world of high-level riding.

For their success in competition, equestrian governance, and life in general, Karen and David are the golden couple of American eventing, role models recognized around the world and swarmed by fans wherever they go.

Although they pursue an expensive sport (for which they're lucky enough to have generous sponsors), neither came from wealth or from a family with a long history of prominent equestrian involvement. They started out as ordinary riding enthusiasts and had as many downs as ups. But they have come to stand out—as riders and as human beings—because of the talent, determination, and plain hard work that have put them far ahead of the pack.

In this book, they'll tell you how they've done it. We won't begin at the beginning, though. Let's start with the achievement that engraved the name O'Connor in the annals of the sport—David's 2000 Olympic gold medal.

Nancy Jaffer
June 2004

CHAPTER ONE

Waving the Stars and Stripes in Sydney

The Gold Medal

SOMETIMES DESTINY boils down to just one crucial moment: a surreal second or two when the world seems to stop, waiting to see what you will do. That instant can make or break you; it's the difference between becoming a star, with your name in the record books, and being known forever as the guy who blew his shot at glory.

For me, David O'Connor, that crossroads moment came in the middle of the show-jumping arena at the 2000 Olympic Games in Sydney, Australia. The stands were packed with twenty thousand people, an ocean of mostly Australian faces, many undoubtedly waiting to see if I might make a mistake. That would open the door for their favorite equestrian son, Andrew Hoy, to win an individual gold medal, providing some nice company for the team gold medal he and his fellow Aussies had earned a few days earlier at the biggest Games on earth. But I was determined to give the USA a good shot at the ultimate prize.

I was leading going into this finale, the last leg of a grueling effort that also included dressage and cross-country jumping in a decisive test of horse and rider. You'd think a horse that had gone cross-country over the most impossible-looking obstacles the day before would be able to ace a few striped poles, a wall or two, and a gate in show jumping. After all, the fences are set up at reasonable heights in a big arena where the ground is level and manicured. But the importance of what's at stake complicates the fact that, unlike the cross-country jumps, the poles of the stadium fences are easily dislodged. Penalty points add up all too easily; with the mere flick of a hoof, a medal can be gone on a tumbling rail.

Though I'm usually pretty good with pressure situations, I was really worried this time around. My horse, Custom Made, had a history of not being the best show jumper. I still flinch remembering how he was eliminated in the show-jumping phase of the Open European Championships in 1995, just a few months after winning Rolex Kentucky with 10 jumping penalties and 1.5 time penalties, taking the honors by a mere, too-close-for-comfort, 0.1 penalties.

In Sydney, I had earned an Olympic-record dressage score of 29 penalties (the fewer penalties, the better) to take the lead, and I kept my edge through cross-country. As the leader, I went last in stadium, the final round of the day. I'd had a lot of conversations with myself the previous night and before I went into the ring. In fact, when I'd stood on the podium during the team medal ceremonies several days earlier—after our US squad won the bronze—I was already in another place, thinking about the individual competition that was to come.

Sport psychology is a big part of what I do. To begin with, of course, you have to get yourself into a frame of mind where the competition means a lot. On the other hand, you can't start thinking that it means a lot about you personally. That kind of separation is hard to do. But, because things aren't always going to work your way, you've got to plan your reaction so you're able to deal with disappointment, and not make it a life-crushing experience when they don't. No matter what happens, if you win it or lose it, you're going to be the same person when you walk out of that ring.

So I thought about how it would be if I didn't get a medal at all, or if I wound up with the bronze or the silver. And I also gave some consideration to what getting the gold would mean—though I kind of figured that one would take care of itself. I knew any of those scenarios could happen, and I wanted to be prepared to handle whatever came along.

I'd had a lot of time to think about everything. We walked the course at 10:00 a.m., but I didn't actually show-jump until 3:00 p.m. During the hours in between, the tension built. I watched the other competitors ride and came up with an inescapable conclusion: This was a tough course. It was going to be particularly hard for Custom Made, I knew. We had generally not finished within the time allowed on show-jumping courses during his career—and being slow carries penalties, too, though not as many as knocking down a jump. A combination of even one knockdown with the wrong number of time faults could be fatal to my aspirations.

When I finally got on and began warming up, Custom Made was jumping OK, and I started to think things would be all right. Then he dropped a rail at each of the four fences that I took. Was he trying too hard? Quickly, a helper set up a smaller, narrower fence, and we cleared it just seconds before we trotted toward the stadium.

I wasn't feeling fantastic. Although I couldn't see what was going on in the main ring, I could hear the crowd roaring in delight; then the sound system blared out that Andrew had jumped a clear round. He moved up from fourth to second when two-time Olympic individual gold medalist Mark Todd of New Zealand, who had been right behind me, scored 3 time penalties and dropped back to third. Andrew and his mount, Swizzle In, were so good that I could afford only two knockdowns. Any more errors than that, and the gold would belong to Andrew.

So I knew, walking in there, what I had to do. There was a lot of applause as the crowd caught sight of me and Custom Made (whom we'd nicknamed Tailor, as in a custom-made suit). Though most of the fans were rooting for Andrew, I also think the clapping signified an appreciation of what Tailor and I had done to that point—and of what else we had to do to get that gold medal.

I cantered all the way from one end of the ring to the other before making the preparatory circle that would lead me to the first jump. What I was doing involved trying to get control of my horse. Tailor had always been nervous in front of big crowds for the show jumping—though, strangely enough, not for the dressage.

While I took a deep breath and a quick glance around, looking for the line I was going to ride to the first fence, I skipped something that's my usual procedure—giving the course one last run-through in my mind. Instead of taking a mental tour of the route in this vast arena, I was concentrating on trying to get Tailor over that first fence because my experience in the schooling area had made me very wary. As it turned out, that omission nearly did me in.

I didn't take any chances. I tried everything, using my legs and rein pressure to help lift Tailor. He jumped the first fence well, and I felt as if our lines of communication were open. He really listened when we made the 180-degree turn to the second jump.

Then came a big test: the third jump, a substantial oxer, or spread fence, that was very square and very wide. It was over on the rail, near the crowd—a location that generally makes Tailor nervous. I helped him off the ground and he exploded over it, nearly jumping me out of the saddle. So I steadied him, and myself, after that. We did well handling the next vertical to an oxer, despite my fears he might get aggressive there.

Then there was an option at number 6: You could take a narrow fence and make a right-hand turn to a wall, which was the longer way, or try two square oxers over liverpools. Only two or three people took that route, and they all had rails down. So I decided on the first option: going over that tall, straight-up-and-down green gate. I hit a good stride to it, but Custom Made knocked it behind—and, for an instant, I listened to hear if the gate had fallen. That's a classic mistake, something you're taught early on in your riding lessons never to do, and the error that had the potential for deep-sixing my gold-medal hopes.

That mental backward glance blanked out my mind. I looked ahead, only to find I wasn't where I'd thought I was. The first fence I saw was a big yellow oxer in front of me. And I was like "Nope, that's not it."

I turned my head, swiveling to find the right fence. That got everyone in the stands gasping, from my wife and teammate, Karen, to US Equestrian Team Coach Mark Phillips and the thousands of spectators whose names I'd never know—but who doubtless would never forget me now, one way or the other.

They thought I was lost.

Truthfully, you do get into a time warp for that moment of panic when you don't know what your next decision is. You're saying, "Wait a minute; where's the next fence?" But while everyone else may have seen the prize slipping away, my thoughts didn't go as far as "Oh my God, I'm about to blow the Olympic gold medal." I was just desperately trying to find where I should be going.

Happily, after what seemed an eternity, I did locate the wall I should be jumping next and headed for it. And although time felt as if it was prancing by in slow motion, it wasn't; with a jolt, I realized that I was running late. With the clock ticking, I really galloped and cut the corner, jumping way on the left-hand side of the wall to make up ground as I saw the prospect of time penalties looming.

I didn't waste a second thinking about my near-mishap as I concentrated on beating the clock. I needed to make small turns that were less time-consuming, and there were only two turns left. We were far from home free. Then came a knockdown at fence 9, a brown vertical that Tailor hit behind—as many times as I've watched the videotape, I still don't know why. With the hardest part of the course coming up, the end of this game definitely was in doubt.

I was worried about the triple combination, fearing Tailor would get aggressive and stop listening to me as he went through it. He handled it, though, and then we had eight or nine strides to the next jump. To avoid having him get too strong, I did what we had planned in our strategy session during the course walk: I took him out of the line and brought him back to it—so he couldn't sight in on the fence and just start a headlong gallop to get there, which would risk the wrong takeoff point and a possible knockdown.

As I cleared that second-to-last jump, I thought, "Wow. I made it through that line." Then it was on to the final barrier between me and the gold medal, a jump featuring the Olympic mascots—Oly, Millie and Syd, little Australian animals who beckoned me home to the finish line. I made a sharp turn, again attempting to tame my time problem. "Just don't blow it now," I told myself. We arced over Oly and his friends, and I galloped for that finish line.

The first thing I did when I crossed it was turn around, looking up at the giant clock on the scoreboard to learn my time. I was one second under the time allowed. No time faults, and only one rail down. We had done it!

Of course, the crowd went crazy. I galloped to the other end of the ring, and suddenly I was deaf to the cheers and applause. It was as if I were in an insulated bubble, where my only thought was "I don't believe it. I just don't believe it." I reached down and patted Tailor. Strangely, it was a quiet moment for me, despite the uproar of the fans. This was it, what I'd been working for. Suddenly, I was a part of history, though I appreciated that it all too easily could have gone the other way.

"Look around," I told myself. "You probably won't ever be here again, like this. Who knows what the future will be?—so appreciate it."

I walked from one end of the ring to the other, taking it all in, after removing my hat to acknowledge the attention from the crowd. Then I looked up and saw Karen going crazy, and I gave a big shrug, like "I don't know what happened in the middle of the course." It was a message from me to her, as if we were the only ones there. She got it, as she always does. After all, I knew she had been jumping every fence with me from her seat.

Of course, the TV guys made the most of my hesitation on course. And at that point I was starting to get mad at myself for that stupid mistake, because it isn't the kind of thing I usually do. I had come so very, very close to losing the medal that was going to be placed around my neck in a few minutes.

As I left the ring, everyone swarmed around me; Karen, Mark and Jim Wolf, the USET's eventing activities director, congratulated me and gave me grief about my little misadventure. My euphoria was lessened a bit by the fact that I hadn't done the job that I wanted. But still, it was a good enough job to win the US the individual gold medal for the first time in twenty-four years, since Tad Coffin did it at the Montreal Games on Bally Cor. I put it all into perspective by realizing that the crucial moment hadn't cost me anything; it didn't detract from the score. So I could live with it, even if I hadn't done the job up to my standard. I had been seriously playing the game and getting pretty cool about it. And really, I had believed that the individual eventing at this Olympics was going to be my competition. It felt as if it was set up for me with that horse, and nobody was going to take it away from me.

But there was little time for those thoughts as I got engulfed in a series of hugs: first from Karen, then from a whole tidal wave of friends and relations. It seemed as if everyone was talking at once.

George Morris, the world-renowned trainer (and Olympic veteran) who'd schooled me for the jumping, knew what it took to get Tailor around that course. "I don't know how you did it," he told me. And, yes indeed, I'm very proud of what we did to get it done, because show jumping wasn't Tailor's strong suit.

Mark said, "David, you gave me a great birthday present." He had just turned fifty-two, and now he had the perfect reason to both swig champagne and start breathing normally again for the first time in months.

Jim Wolf defied the security guards and got an American flag, tied to a crop, out to me for the victory gallop. It was worth his effort. Photos of me carrying the flag as I cantered around the arena were all over TV and made the front page of papers around the world.

Although I look understandably happy in all those pictures, I wasn't swept away by euphoria. You see other people on TV screaming and jumping up and down and losing it when they win a gold medal. That wasn't there—I think because I was still kicking myself. So I went another way. I got quiet. It was kind of just me and my horse; I didn't go crazy. But I did know that life would never be the same, in so many ways that I couldn't even guess about at that moment.

This kind of success puts you into certain roles. When you win a gold medal, people look up to you; it's natural. You either take that role on or you hide from it. There are people who don't like that role for themselves, and I have no problem with that. But if you take that role and see what good things it can do, personally, sport-wise and public-wise, I think you can enjoy it.

People all want to feel good about themselves. There are people who take the people around them and put them down, and that makes them feel good about themselves; and people who take the people around them and bring them up, and that makes *them* feel good about themselves. I like to bring people up, and I'm very comfortable in that role, but public admiration is not the driving force in my life. The public and private sides need to be balanced, and my private side is very private.

Karen and I do feel we have obligations, though, and one of them is meeting with the public and signing autographs, as we do at every event, even if we're tired or have had a bad day. What's twenty minutes? We can spare it. We realize that if we take the time, those people will be fans—not just of ours, but of the sport—for the rest of their lives. We take our roles in the equestrian world very seriously. There are children everywhere who read stories about us, or see our photos. We have something they admire, and maybe they want to be successful in the same way we are. That puts us in a position of power, not that we asked for it, of course. Still, we feel strongly that any position of power means you have to be responsible, and that if you're irresponsible, you lose that sparkle in the eye of a kid who wanted to emulate you. It's important to us to help make good citizens who become good adults and good parents, because being with horses impacts a child's whole life.

Karen and I know what it's like to be on the other side of things, to ask for an autograph or a minute of a riding superstar's time. Both of us started as what most people call "backyard" riders. To some, that's a derogatory term for being small-time. But working with our horses ourselves, caring for them, mucking stalls, trail riding, and just having fun in the saddle paid off. It made us horse people, not just riders. And eventing isn't like many other riding sports, where you can hop on a well-trained horse, do your thing, hop off, and hand the reins to a groom as you go look for your next ride. Conditioning and knowing your horses—intimately—are keys to success in eventing.

So let us tell you how we got started, and you'll see what we mean.

Remembering a Course

At some point, it happens to everybody. You're jumping a course, and suddenly you go blank. Where is the next fence? As you fight a rising tide of panic, your momentary lapse may have you circling, stopping, or jumping the wrong obstacle, which means elimination.

Preparation and focus are your best weapons against a moment that at best is embarrassing and at worst can cost you a major competition.

When you're walking the course, break it down into segments, the jumping equivalent of bite-size pieces. Then put them all together. After you've walked the course as many times as possible, go over it again and again in your head through visualization. You can say it to yourself, then close your eyes and picture it in your mind, like a movie. As you watch, see your horse doing his best. Visualize yourself doing it nicely.

Go over it one more time as you ride into the arena: before you salute if possible, or right afterwards if they're rushing you. Don't skip this important step. Look at each of the fences in the order in which you will take them, and feel each click into your head.

Once you make your circle and head for the first fence, start thinking in slow motion so there's enough time to do everything. As soon as you start allowing things to happen very quickly in your mind, you don't have enough time to prepare for everything. If you're watching the show *ER* on TV and a group of victims come into the hospital, things are moving very fast in slow motion. The doctor might be doing things rapidly, but his brain is working methodically and systematically and, in effect, slowly, so there's enough time not to forget anything.

Keep in touch with the horse's direction, speed, balance, and rhythm as you go along. Never think about what's behind you; always think about what's in front of you. Never think what's happened; always think what's happening and what's going to happen. If you glance back, physically or mentally, to the previous fence while you're on course, you run the risk of losing your concentration on your job and forgetting where you're going. You'll have plenty of time to rehash which rails fell after you leave the arena.

CHAPTER TWO

Ready for my first cross-country, literally!

Starting Out

I GOT INVOLVED with horses because of my mother, Sally, who was and still is very immersed in the equestrian world. She had ponies as a girl and wanted her children to have them, too, though her background was quite different from ours.

Mom grew up in a suburban area of England, the daughter of an insurance executive. She came over to the US in 1957, working her way around the world. She met my father, Jay, at a reception while she was working as a secretary in Washington, D.C. He was a naval engineer, originally from upstate New York; but his mother, who was a maid, and his dad, who worked for the railroad, had come over from Ireland.

My father had graduated from the New York Maritime School and was selected to go in the naval submarine service as a reserve officer. What we know about what he did after that—he designed top-secret stuff for submarines—I can sum up by saying that he rose as high as a civilian could in the Navy department.

After we moved out to Gaithersburg, Maryland, from suburban Bethesda, Mom went to work in the office at the nearby Potomac Horse Center. That's when our life with horses really began. We started to take lessons at Potomac, which was run at that time by Lockie Richards, a native of New Zealand. I was only six, but I still remember Flying Fortress and Bramanmoor, the first horse I ever cantered on. My brother, Brian, who's two and a half years older than I am, got a pony named Bramble when he was ten; and when I turned ten, I wound up with that feisty little mare. (You could say Bramble and I had an up-and-down relationship at the beginning. One of my first memories of her was of getting on at the barn and having her run off to the house with me. Then she put her head down to eat the lawn as I screamed and yelled for Mom to help me.)

Dad built a barn in the backyard, which was pretty spacious. Our neighborhood was so large that you had to ride a horse or a bicycle to get to your friends' houses. We joined the Redland Hunt Pony Club, but we also played football and baseball.

Though the only showing we did was locally, Mom got active in Pony Club and became the local District Commissioner. She even started a little event. The first time I rode in it was not a good portent for my equestrian future: I got eliminated in the dressage when my pony ran right out of the ring.

I didn't have "the" competitive horse when I was young. I never did the A-rated circuit or even outside events. Still, I was able to get a glimpse of that world. Eight-time Olympian Mike Plumb lived in Maryland and used to lecture; Mom was so involved in the equestrian scene that we got Mike and people like him to come to our Pony Club and help us.

One summer, Brian and I spent a couple of weeks with friends who raised horses. That's when I broke my arm, after Bramble dumped me. It was to be the first of many horse-related injuries. I also broke my collarbone at one point in my childhood, but I wasn't discouraged. Being afraid never even crossed my mind. Not only do I have a high tolerance for pain but, luckily, I never connected getting hurt with being afraid of riding.

Any riding success I had came quite late. I have to say that as a kid I never thought about being a professional rider. I was always interested in space and considered a career as an astronaut, as many kids do. (I've abandoned most of those fantasies, of course, but I will get my pilot's license someday, because flying holds great fascination for me.)

Even though I wasn't thinking about making the Olympic team, I was still exposed early to the Olympic concept. My mother competed at the international level; and we went to the Fair Hill event in Maryland in 1971, where Brian was the gatekeeper for dressage. So I was around the Olympians and top pros. We have a photo of my brother with Olympic medalist Jimmy Wofford and his horse, Kilkenny, from back then; at the time, I never dreamed what a big influence Jimmy—now coach of the Canadian team—would be in my life.

My father was always supportive, though he's not a horse person. Now he's gotten to the point where he can at least hold horses; back then, though, he traveled a lot and didn't go to many events. That was Mom's deal.

By the early 1970s, my folks were doing their separate things; they didn't get along very well, and that part was very hard. We weren't so much a family unit as four individuals.

Meanwhile, I wasn't having much luck with horses. Bramble was put down because she was a carrier of Equine Infectious Anemia, a disease that hit our area in the early 1970s. My next horse, Hobbit, another hand-me-down from my brother, also had to be euthanized as an EIA carrier. But first she taught me a bit about training. She didn't have a good trot, so I'd canter her first; that seemed to fix it. I was on to something as I started thinking—in an elementary way initially, of course—

about techniques that could improve my mounts' way of going.

Next, a neighbor loaned us a pony called Sonny, whom I got along with quite well. We were the same age, and this pony lived to be thirty-eight. He was still alive when I was at the Atlanta Olympics, and he sent me a note (probably written by his owners) when we medaled there.

After Sonny, I had a little gray mare. We were jumping one day and she pulled up lame behind, so we sent her to the University of Pennsylvania's New Bolton clinic. She came back after they checked her out and didn't find anything, but it turned out she had a spiral fracture. After she came back to our farm, she snapped her leg in half while grazing. I was fourteen and the only one home at the time. I called the vet, then stayed with her for a couple of hours until he came to put her down. It was a devastating afternoon, but I felt at least I had comforted her in her final moments. Learning how to deal with having a horse die was something I would have to do, because it's part of a life with horses.

Interestingly, the turning point of my childhood riding career didn't involve showing or eventing. Instead, it was all about a journey across the country that my mother, my brother, and I made. You may have heard about it, because the trip has become legendary. Most people wonder "What were you thinking?" to even imagine undertaking a journey like that, but at the time it just seemed like a fun idea—especially for a young kid.

One night when I was nine, Brian and Mom got into conversation over dinner about Thor Heyerdahl's book *Kon-Tiki*, which he wrote after crossing the ocean on a raft. Brian said, "Wouldn't it be neat to do something like this?" No way on a boat, of course, but Mom got an idea. She took the bit in her teeth and was off and running.

"What about riding to California?" she asked us casually. Because she's British and grew up on John Wayne movies, she'd always wanted to see the fabled American West. Adding fuel to her fire was the fact that she had just read a book called *The Tale of Two Horses* by Aime Tschiffely, about a guy who rode from Buenos Aires to Washington, D.C. My parents were splitting up about then, too, and I guess that was part of her motivation to get away.

That's how it started, and the more people said it couldn't be done, the more Mom decided it should be done; it *had* to be done. If she had stayed in Britain, where she was born, she would have been the formidable matriarch of a large family. She's very forceful in her personality. However, she is not what I would call an optimist by nature, while I very much am. You see, the British are not happy unless there's a stressful situation. Mom particularly prefers one in which she can take charge, like the ride.

I guess you've figured out that we're a family of contrasts. Brian has always been funny and outgoing. He can walk into any group, and within thirty minutes he's entertaining them and they're all laughing. I can do that for *my* people, if I'm there for a reason, but not if there's a crowd of strangers. When my parents split, Brian became even more of an extrovert, but I turned inward.

On the trip, our personalities were reflected in how we rode. Brian would always be in the front, the pathfinder. My mother would be second, holding the fort, and I would bring up the rear, often in my own world. Also, I was only ten years old, going on eleven, so I was definitely a follower.

I don't believe Mom ever thought I would be the real rider in the family. I think she always expected Brian to be the rider—because when he was younger, he worked harder at it than I did. After it became evident that that was the way I was going, though, she was good about it. She supported my career but didn't push, though she loved it when I rode in England at Badminton and Burghley, because that was her dream. It became very apparent early on that while I appreciated her opinion— which is especially important because she's a dressage judge—I didn't want her as a coach. That was hard, because she was interested in being a big

23

part of what I did, and it took a lot of self-restraint on her part not to interfere. I'm happy to say that we worked it out. The trip gave us a good foundation for understanding. It was so important in enabling us to gain respect for each other and setting up the parameters that would be the guideposts in our relationship for the rest of our lives. It also gave us common ground and a common goal.

The three of us were already bonding more deeply as we prepared to leave, having fun conversations about what would go in our saddlebags when they were finally made for us. We went to the headquarters of *National Geographic* to get the appropriate maps. After poring over them, we decided to go to Oregon instead of California, because we wanted to avoid the desert, and the Oregon Trail followed rivers.

Mom was busy lining up places where we could stop and give the horses a break along the way. Dressage trainer Kay Meredith was a crony of hers, so we were going to her place, Meredith Manor in West Virginia. Mom also knew a fellow named George Glass in Indiana; and she had a friend from eventing, Charles "Chick" Chapin, in Springfield, Illinois. The only other person she had a contact with out West was Lowell Boomer, founder of the US Dressage Federation, in Lincoln, Nebraska.

So, basically, we were about to take a big leap into the unknown: a feeling that I now can compare to my first takeoff from a big cross-country bank jump. But hey, it was an adventure, and we were more than ready to go.

"Gassing up" somewhere along the Oregon Trail

The Trip

WHEN WE OUTLINED the trip, we figured that we'd hit our "oasis" stables every ten days and take a little time there to rest after going an average of thirty to thirty-five miles a day and camping out at night. It was an ambitious agenda—and, needless to say, things didn't always go as planned. The whims of terrain and weather meant we didn't always get as far as we wanted to go during each stretch. On some days, our mileage was only in the teens; on our longest day, it was an amazing forty-eight miles.

I was riding a horse called Ralph, lent to us by Ray Little, a Maryland horse and trailer dealer whose wife Lynne and daughter Marilyn now are grand prix show-jumping stars. Brian was on B.G., a neighbor's horse, and Mom was aboard her event horse, Gung Ho. We'd had a few days of trial runs, getting the horses used to packing our gear by riding around the neighborhood. I remember a bucking-bronco session when Ralph decided he didn't like being a packhorse: You realize you haven't packed well when everything falls in a rain of stuff from the saddlebags.

Unlike the pioneers whose path we followed to some extent, we rode in English saddles, with sleeping bags tied behind them. Basically all we carried was a change of clothing, rain ponchos that could double as tents, ropes, a set of farrier's tools, food, and a harmonica we didn't know how to play. Across my lap I balanced a nylon duffel bag full of oats. (Because I was the lightest, I had to carry the most weight.)

We set out on May 13, 1973—which, appropriately, was Mother's Day—from White's Ferry in Maryland, on the towpath of the C&O Canal. The canal, a project started by George Washington, goes straight west, which is where we were headed. Friends came down to see us off, as did several newspaper reporters and photographers. And then we started riding.

At the end of that momentous first day, after we completed our thirty miles, friends came down to meet us and brought along food, which we ate both ravenously and gratefully. I remember one of my mother's pals saying, "This is the way you should do the whole thing. You should have it catered."

I'll never forget that night, because I was sore: rubbed raw from new jeans we hadn't washed before we set off. Boy, was that a big mistake—and far from the only one we were to make on our journey.

Once the horses finished eating from nosebags, we turned them out in an eight-acre field. That led to learning experience number two: Next morning, even though they'd had all night to eat and relax, they apparently were reluctant to head down the trail again. It took us three frustrating hours to catch them. So the next night we tied them to a tree. That did not turn out to be the best solution to the problem; in the morning, we found they had wound their ropes all around the trunk and were stuck tighter than ticks. We hadn't yet learned the wisdom of the old maxim "Tie horses high and dogs low."

Naturally, sibling rivalry reared its head during our trip.

Brian had a good laugh when I fell asleep in the saddle in West Virginia and woke up on the ground after the too-loose girth slipped. I had to wait a long time, but Brian got his come-uppance, and I got my laugh in Wyoming. On that portion of our ride, he was the one who didn't check his girth and hit the deck after his saddle went sideways. We still share a chuckle about those mishaps today, but they taught me a lesson I never forgot. I always check my girth several times during a ride, even today.

But those mishaps were nothing compared to other situations we were to face. Real trouble found us early on. One of the stone aqueducts across the river was only six feet wide, and there was no way to get around it. The only alternative was backtracking seventy miles. So we wound up getting off the horses and gingerly walking them across the narrow top, making sure we didn't look down. Those hair-raising moments atop the aqueduct really impressed on us that this trip was going to be a challenge, not a lark.

We found ourselves doing a lot of problem-solving along the way, but there were also unexpected bonuses. By now we were in West Virginia, on the edge of Route 50. By four or five o'clock in the afternoon each day, we'd start knocking on doors of farmhouses, looking for a place to stay. We'd tell people what we were doing; when they recovered from their surprise, many of them invited us to spend the night. We usually asked to sleep in the barn, but often they'd insist we sleep in the house, in real beds that were quite a treat for us after curling up in sleeping bags. These stops were an opportunity for me to relax a little bit; I was always hopping up on a tractor or playing with the other kids we met along the way. In the course of our door-knocking, we only got turned down three times.

You know, the fact that we were a mother and her two kids on their own made a lot of people very protective of us. And most of them could not believe what we were doing. "You're from *where?*" they'd ask incredulously. "And you're going *where?*"

When we weren't lucky enough to find a hospitable farmhouse, we'd sleep along the road at a rest stop, lying down as best we could on picnic tables. One night, some people drag-racing at 3:00 or 4:00 in the morning scared the horses and we worried about them trying to high-tail it home. On another evening the horses got loose in a thunderstorm and were racing around like mad before we managed to round them up, all of us a lot soggier for the experience.

We'd had a few such "rest stop" nights before reaching Meredith Manor, so it was a welcome pit stop when we finally reached it. We met a bunch of college kids there, which was fun, and it was nice to sleep in real beds and have stalls for the horses. We also took this opportunity to get the horses shod. Because we'd been traveling on paved roads a great deal of the time, their shoes were so thin that you could bend them in half.

From West Virginia, we went into Ohio, where it rained every afternoon as we trotted uncomfortably past the pig farms and soybean fields. In Chillicothe, we rode into a drive-in restaurant and ordered as if we were in a car. When the waitress came out with our meal, she went into shock and nearly dropped the food. Actually, I'm surprised she didn't see more people on horses, since it was the summer of the gasoline embargo and endless lines at filling stations. Some of the people who drove by us probably were envious that our transportation ran on oats.

Our trip was a low-budget operation. We rode into a lot of towns without money in our pockets, but people always took care of us. As we went on, things got better, because our trip received publicity and folks knew we were coming, so they'd look out for us.

In Nebraska, where we were on one road the whole way, the police came out one night to deliver a message that some people had invited us to stay with them. Their place was a little off the highway, and by the time we neared the turnoff, it was dark. We exited from the highway onto a narrow, two-lane bridge. For some reason, I was in front for a change. Then this tractor-trailer came rolling up. The driver didn't see me until he was so close that he had no chance to slow down. The truck went rolling by me at 70 mph. The horses, however, didn't miss a beat. That was lucky, since there was a four-hundred-foot drop into a gully from the ramp; if they had spooked, it would have been all over. I will never forget seeing the rivets on that tractor-trailer as it went by. That's how close he was.

That was probably our most dangerous moment, but there were other times of great uncertainty, like getting lost in the Rocky Mountains, where we wound up staying with sheepherders.

We kept in contact with Dad by calling collect to tell him where we were. He had a map of the US in his office; using thumbtacks, he followed our progress by marking all the places we'd been.

This trip was life-altering for so many obvious reasons. But the biggest thing it did for me, from a character point of view, was give me a tremendous amount of respect for how people live. We stayed with both very poor people and very wealthy people. No matter where I go in the world, I get along with folks because I have so much respect for what they do. I don't believe that one job is lower than another job; that's just not in my makeup, and a lot of that mindset is from the trip. I have a job that has a very high profile, but other people with other jobs are just as serious about the things they do—whatever they are—as I am about what I do. The difference is that I picked a very public format—and when I make a mistake, everybody talks about it for a long time.

Another thing the trip taught me was to be a problem-solver. For a young kid, I took on a lot of responsibility. That impressed on me the importance of taking charge and following through. That's why, later in life, I volunteered to become the first president of the US Equestrian Federation, which is something I'll tell you more about a little later.

During the trip, though, because I really was just a little boy, I sometimes had difficulty dealing with my emotions along the way. By the time we rode into Nebraska, for example, my horse had developed an infected wither because that bag of oats I was carrying was rubbing on him, despite a six-inch foam pad that we'd hoped would relieve the pressure. A guy named Ellis Ruby, who ran a big Arabian breeding farm in Scottsbluff, and whom we met when we just knocked on his door, suggested I leave Ralph there and take one of his six hundred horses. He lent me a horse who was half-Arab/half-Thoroughbred, and we went on our way. I cried for two days because the horse wasn't Ralph, with whom I had bonded by now. We soon found, however, that this little horse was very useful and clever; I wound up naming him Jim Bridger, after the frontiersman. One day I was the scout when we hit an area that had been logged. The trail had been lost in the process, but Jim the horse was so careful as we picked our way around the timber that I was in awe of him. At one stop in Illinois, we put the horses in a small barn with a low doorframe. Mom's horse jumped as he was led in and cracked his back. We nursed the injury for fifteen hundred miles, Mom riding with a thick foam pad we got from a bedding store. But the morning we set out from Torrington, Wyoming, we hadn't gone more than fifteen miles before it was obvious that Gung Ho was really hurting.

A t that point, uncharacteristically, Mom decided we should quit the whole project and go home; she was very concerned for her horse. With Brian, she hitchhiked back to where we had been the night before, to get help, while I stayed behind and took care of the horses.

However, when some people in this little Wyoming town heard Mom's tale and learned she couldn't go on, they contacted neighbors who loaned her a four-year-old, semi-broke chestnut mare. They even refused to take Gung Ho as collateral, so we sent him back to the Arabian farm and continued to Oregon.

One of the reasons that people were so nice to us is, I think, that they wanted something to believe in. They wanted to believe in a mother and two children trying to ride from one side of the country to another, basically for no reason. And they wanted to be sure we made it.

We did get to Oregon, though we never reached the Pacific as we originally planned. Brian and I had to be back in school that September, and we basically ran out of time. Someone we had met along the way drove to Oregon and picked up the horses, dropping them off with Ralph in Scottsbluff. We took the bus home: a bit of an anticlimax after our ride, but a far quicker way of covering the ground between us and Maryland. Later, a cross-country shipper picked up our horses and brought them home. B.G. had made it all the way to Oregon and back. We sold Jim to a friend of ours as a Pony Club horse.

The trip gave me fodder for a great essay about "What I did on my summer vacation." But, as I've already told you, it meant far more to me than that. As I look back, I can see how so much of what I am today came from that extraordinary journey. It taught me how to be self-reliant and self-entertained. We didn't have a Walkman or anything like that to occupy our minds. We just talked to each other and our horses, did a lot of thinking, and appreciated the country. I learned great respect for people and this land—and more than anything else, perhaps, the virtues of plodding on against the odds.

The trip cemented my relationship with my mother and brother because we went through so many difficult and semi-dangerous things together, kind of the way soldiers become lifelong friends in a war. Brian and I are very, very close. I can compare it to being on an Olympic team, now that I know what that's like, because by the time you get where you're going, you've jumped through a thousand hoops together.

It was a fascinating odyssey for so many reasons—but most of all because my mother had the strength of character to go, and because I gained so much as a result. I think about it all the time, especially when

31

I'm traveling the world in the luxury of a 747 or a limo. It's at those moments that I appreciate how much the trip, which once just seemed like such a crazy idea, was one of the reasons I got where I am today.

INSIGHT

It's a Small World After All

Both Karen and I are fascinated by what *horses* do, not just by what event horses do. I think that, in the end, we all wind up speaking one language with the horse as we solve his problems and try to get him to work with us.

Horses don't think differently because they're Trakehners or Paso Finos or Appaloosas. They all process information very similarly, rather than in a breed-specific way, even though they may have differences in temperament and way of going.

We think there's a lot to learn from other disciplines. What about the mental partnership that the Western guys have with their Quarter Horses—that quietness and understanding of the job that those horses as a general rule display, as well as the lack of anxiety about the work they do?

Of course, there are many distinctions among the breeds and disciplines when you get down to the fine points. Hop on a cutting horse and he makes a dressage horse look dead on his feet. That extreme sensitivity is fascinating to feel. A cutting or reining horse is much more sensitive to the aids than most dressage and jumping horses. Those disciplines don't worry about quality of movement, however. On the other hand, we don't need to go to a cutting or reining horse's level of sensitivity and extreme lightness because we have to worry more about the elasticity of the movements.

We don't like the fact that in the English world we're generally not taught about what the horse is thinking, but only about what the horse is doing. When we discuss round-pen work or other "horse whisperer" concepts, what it does is open a door to starting to consider what the horse is thinking and why he reacts in certain ways. I think that helps us with everything we do in our life with horses.

My childhood ride across the country and going out West to work a few years later gave me an appreciation for all the Western stuff, but Karen did a lot of riding breed-specific horses. She showed Morgans, Tennessee Walkers, and Connemaras. Between the two of us there's always been an appreciation for people who were doing other things with horses. That gave us a respect for the level of excellence in a lot of different disciplines while we were specializing in what interested us.

In the broader picture, we feel just as comfortable in a tuxedo or evening gown as in muck boots and shorts. We've done everything from having tea at Buckingham Palace to going out with a group of Polish peasant farmers who didn't speak our language but who showed us a good time. We feel at home at both ends of the spectrum, and there's no doubt in our minds that our involvement with horses, in all their manifestations, is what has enabled us to do that.

CHAPTER FOUR

Competing at Bialy Bor, Poland, with Border Raider

Getting Serious

WHEN I WAS SIXTEEN, I got my first competition horse, Blue Monday. He had done Preliminary eventing with his former owner, a Young Rider, and we bought him for $4,000, which was a lot of money in those days—especially for us. I was excited about doing my first three-day event, at Radnor, Pennsylvania, with him. But I fell at the first steeplechase fence, and Blue Monday ran off. Then he tied up, a type of muscle cramping that was an awful ending to a terrible day, and hardly an auspicious beginning to my career in the sport.

Softening the blow, good things also were happening for me on the eventing front. This was 1978, the year of the World Championships at the new Kentucky Horse Park in Lexington, and I'd gotten hooked up with the New Zealand team because Lockie Richards, my mother's old trainer from Potomac, was their coach. They were training in the States and needed grooms, so my brother and I volunteered. I worked for Carol Harrison, who ended up sixth.

Also on that New Zealand team was a promising rider named Mark Todd, a lanky fellow who would go on to win two individual Olympic gold medals with that plucky little one-of-a-kind horse, Charisma. When I won my individual gold medal at the 2000 Olympics, Mark was on the podium, too, receiving a bronze medal. It was the end of his career in eventing; he was retiring to train racehorses. I like thinking that I was there for the beginning and the end of the international eventing run of one of the greatest riders the sport has ever known.

The 1978 championships marked my first real hands-on interaction at an event of this magnitude, and it was awesome. I had been to the 1974 World Championships in England with my mother; but because I was only twelve, I didn't get the full impact of what it meant.

The year after the Championships in Kentucky, I went to the old Essex Horse Trials on the US Equestrian Team's property in Gladstone, New Jersey, and had a couple of refusals at one of the most hallowed landmarks in the horse world. Luckily for my morale, things were better a few months later at Radnor, in the Harry T. Peters Trophy for the Young Rider Championships, which were a huge deal at that point. I wound up second, with just a couple of rails down in show jumping between me and that shiny silver souvenir. But the best part was that, finally, I had a chance to serve notice that I was a potential contender for serious eventing honors.

I was in high school at the time and very much involved in music and singing. I was a soloist at St. Peter's, a church on Capitol Hill in Washington, D.C. I enjoyed musicals and I studied acting—not in formal classes, but more by paying attention to actors' techniques. (As a result, I can do a little acting when I need to. That's come in quite handy in the horse world many times, believe me.)

At this point, I was trying to figure out what I would do for the rest of my life, and I thought about being a singer. I also briefly contemplated being a veterinarian. I didn't consider horses as part of my livelihood, however, because we couldn't afford what it would take to set me up in the horse business.

I got to conduct in concerts at the end of my senior year, and I also did a little bit of teaching. This would prove to be an important time for me, as I learned from my music courses the leadership skills that would figure prominently in my career.

I kept riding, too, and in 1981 I finally made it to the big Rolex Kentucky event—though I was just in the Preliminary section. It didn't go well, however. I had a bad fall, flipping off Blue Monday and breaking both my arms, shattering my left and sustaining a vertical break in my right. I had to be flown out of there by helicopter: a dramatic exit. Amazingly, I made it back to the Kentucky Horse Park for the competitors' party that night. Demerol, the painkiller they gave me, worked great. And that was when I met Karen.

Our meeting wasn't an ideal situation, though, like you envision when you hear the song "Some Enchanted Evening." As you probably can imagine, I didn't look so good across that crowded room, with one arm in a sling and the other strapped across my chest. I certainly made quite an impression on Karen, though; the first time she saw me, I'm told, she said, "Who the heck is *that* guy?" She has since informed me that I was dancing with two really good-looking women at the same time, but I've got to take her word for it, since I don't remember anything about that night.

That fall, I was supposed to head off to Jimmy Wofford's place in Virginia to ride, but my horse went lame at the Chesterland event in Pennsylvania just before that. I was very disappointed until Jimmy suggested I come anyway and help him on the farm. He loves to tell the story about the day he went on a trip and left me in charge, with orders to mow the field. I decided to get creative and etch my initials in the grass with big sweeps of the mower. What I didn't know was that as I made my mark, he was in a plane, flying above the farm. He saw what I was doing, giving him the ammo for quite a lecture when he returned. He's gotten a lot of mileage out of that tale in dinner-party speeches over the years.

I've been strongly influenced by Jimmy, an incredibly intelligent and well-read guy. He taught me a lot about long-term planning. From him, I also learned about the ability to detach yourself and not let your emotions get tied up. He plays little games with people, something I don't do. But I must admit I've studied his methods. Most people who talk to him believe, "He looks at you like he knows what you're thinking." Actually, he doesn't have a clue. It's just a technique that makes people nervous, so they spill the beans.

Jimmy and I rarely talk about horses in depth, though. We're both interested in so many other things that we have some pretty intense, wide-ranging conversations.

After working for Jimmy, I went to England for a year with $300 and a plane ticket, nothing more. Luckily, my mother still had family and friends over there that I could stay with. In London, I sold chocolates at Harrod's, the famous department store. But I was longing to get out in the countryside, so I got some jobs helping veterinarians. I did a lambing in Scotland, where we delivered about six hundred lambs. For the rest of the year, I worked on farms and loved it.

When I came home, I spent some time, off and on, at a community college attached to the University of Maryland. I was studying pre-vet stuff, but I didn't think I'd make it, since my grades were only B's. It's harder to get into veterinary school than medical school in this country, because there are fewer universities that offer vet training.

So I wasn't sure which way to go until I got a letter in 1981 from Jack Le Goff, the Frenchman who was the US Equestrian Team's eventing coach. He invited me to join the next January's developing-rider training sessions, which he held in different places across the country.

This was an important moment, one of two that changed my life over the next decade. Any time you got a letter from the USET and Jack was a big deal. I thought this could be a career opening for me, especially since I'd realized when I got back from England—where I hadn't ridden at all—that horses were something I wanted to be a big part of my life.

Of course, I only had a little Novice-level five-year-old at the time, so I had to borrow a horse for the session with Jack at the USET training center in South Hamilton, Massachusetts. It was a ten-day stint, during which we rode once a day for two hours, with lectures on riding and stable management in between. The program was very theoretical, very methodical, and very cavalry-oriented. I had to learn to keep my mouth shut—another good lesson.

Packy McGaughan, who went on to ride in Indiana on the 1987 Pan American Games gold-medal squad and get an individual bronze medal there, was the resident rider at South Hamilton. However, as another outspoken guy, he was having such a hard time with the situation that he left. Meanwhile, I had gone home after my ten days were up; I didn't know where I was going or what I was doing.

One moody night, my mother and I were speaking about Jack, my training session, and the fact that Packy had packed up and gone. Could that mean an opening for me, I wondered, not knowing what Jack would think about the idea.

"Why don't you just call him?" my mother asked.

So I walked right upstairs and dialed the phone. I'm not a person who usually does something like that, but I rang Jack at his home and said I'd be interested in the job.

I'll never forget what he said. "Boy, you're a ballsy guy. You know, this is my home number, and people don't usually call me at home," he pointed out in his heavily accented English.

Had I done the wrong thing? But there was time for only an instant of doubt, because Jack stopped scolding me and said, "I'll talk to you tomorrow."

He called back the next day and asked me to come up for an interview. It went well, perhaps better than I had a right to expect. You see, I wasn't very skilled at jumping. But he took that in stride.

"You're good on the flat and good with horses, so I'm willing to take a chance with you," he told me.

I was very different from the other people he'd seen—not only because of the jumping thing, but also because I didn't have any money. Still, he glimpsed something in me and took a chance. That started my career, really against the odds.

Things weren't any easier for me, though, despite getting the job. Here's how they stood: I was not being paid, and I drove up there in a rickety 1973 Dodge Duster. I had a Novice horse. I had never ridden above the Preliminary level. I had just turned twenty. There was nothing on paper that said I should be there. Yet it changed my whole life, right then, and gave me a feeling for how to take advantage of possibilities, even if they're long shots. (That's an ability that has come in very, very handy over the years.) The opportunities with which I was presented were exciting, but I knew there was a lot to do to make everything come together.

I was at the USET for four years. Only two other people came during that period for a short time: Cindy Collier for six months and Holly Mitten for two months. The USET actually owned horses back then, something it no longer does, so I was given several to compete. At one point, I got Grey Tudor, an Advanced horse that 1984 Olympic team gold and individual silver medalist Karen Stives used to ride. He took me around my first Intermediate course.

Meanwhile, I was struggling financially. The team gave me a room, and my horse got a stall, but food and salary were not included in the deal. Eventually, though, I made progress, moving up to a small efficiency apartment, and I didn't starve to death. While Jack was gone for the 1982

World Championships in Germany, I taught locally to get spending money and did yard work—first at his house, and then for the team. I made the place look like it should look as part of the USET.

I spruced up everything enough to impress Jimmy Wofford. When he went over to the World Championships, he carried the news about his visit to South Hamilton. "You wouldn't believe what the place looks like," he told Jack.

Jack called from Europe to say, "You're doing a great job." Then he got me hired by the team to be assistant farm manager, so I could get paid, which made my life a little easier.

Finally, I was earning a real living—well, sort of, anyway—but the riding wasn't fantastic. I fell off in a Novice event in front of a big crowd, and it was embarrassing. Here was "the USET rider" hitting the dirt; I was devastated. It got me wondering if I was going to be successful or ever be on a team.

Two-time World Champion Bruce Davidson was the first person out of the Le Goff/USET training system, and I was the last. Bruce, 1976 Olympic gold medalist Tad Coffin, and the others of their era who trained with Jack *had* to ride on a team; that was part of the deal. Luckily, I did not have that kind of pressure.

That doesn't mean I wasn't under the gun, though. By my third year there, I weighed only 138 pounds (I'm 175 now), and I had a tic under one eye. Jack didn't mind ripping into you, and you weren't allowed to respond. I felt I could deal with the fact that what he was saying was important, but how he was saying it was tough to handle.

But though Jack's approach was hard to take, the whole experience was something I wouldn't trade, sort of like being in the French Foreign Legion. (I can still conjure up in my mind how my seat hurt from the many hours of sitting trot that were such a big part of Jack's curriculum.) Despite the tough times, I'm glad I had the opportunity—which isn't available anymore. Jack no longer teaches, and the USET left South Hamilton long ago.

A true master of the sport, Jack was also at the top of his game from an organizational standpoint. He had a cavalry background himself, from France's equestrian training center in Saumur, and his technique was to try to break you down and then build you back up. He did it in a very aggressive way. Your job with Jack was to figure out what he was doing or wanted before he said it. That taught you to be ahead of the game: something that is necessary in competition, and in the rest of life, too, as I've found out.

You see, the sport of eventing is shifting, and you have to keep up with it. Endurance is less of a factor these days than it used to be. Dressage and show jumping are more of a factor. It's not going to do you any good to ride the kind of horse that would have been successful fifteen years ago. You either shift or you get left; you can't sit there and whine about it. That's figuring out what the game is, and that's just reality.

After Jack left the USET in 1984, I stayed another eighteen months at the team farm. Things were getting better for me; I finished seventh at Chesterland, the late lamented Pennsylvania three-star-rated event, in the fall of 1985. The horses I rode included For Kicks, who was bred in the USET program. I won the DeBroke trophy with him, which was a big deal. It built on the success I'd experienced in 1984, when I won Radnor on Kempis, whom Jack had bought from France; he was a nice horse, but a tying-up problem ended his career.

During that time, I was teaching for a woman named Janet Ballentine. She decided she wanted a good event horse, so we went to England and bought Border Raider, who was my first international horse. He was awkward-looking, and Jack hated him at first. But he was a good jumper, so Jack grew to like him. He won the one-star at Radnor in 1984. Then I broke my collarbone on Kempis the next year, so I couldn't ride at Kentucky. Though that was very frustrating, in eventing you get lots of practice dealing with disappointments like that. Later in the season, after I healed, Border Raider was seventh at Chesterland, where Karen won.

Though I fell in the water when we finally got to Kentucky in 1986, the team liked what I was doing, and they sent me to Poland for what amounted to an alternate World Championships. The official World Championships were in Australia that year, and some countries couldn't go; so they needed an event for the nations that weren't able to foot the bill to go Down Under. Of course, the bigger countries—the US and Britain, for instance—sent teams to both events. I, however, rode as an individual and had to pay my own way.

This was a real turning point for me in an exotic locale. I won a silver medal in Poland. More important, though, Karen was competing there, too. It's where we became friends, setting the stage for far more than that in the future.

As it happened, later that year I moved down to Virginia, where Karen was based. Jimmy told me about a farm that was available for rent, so I took it and lived in Upperville for four years. Friendship developed into love as Karen and I started going out in 1987.

So I've told you about my life to this point. Now it's Karen's turn.

Falling Off

There is an art to falling off in such a way that it minimizes your chances of getting hurt, and it's just as important to know about that as it is to learn how to sit the trot properly or get a clean flying change.

When you become unseated, the most important thing you can do is not to stick out your legs or arms. If you try to break your fall, the odds are that what you'll break is a bone.

The second most important thing to remember is to roll away from your horse. You don't want him to fall on you or step on you when he's getting up or running away.

Try to remember the tumbling classes you had when you *(continued)* were little. Every kid has to go through these. They're mandatory because people fall down, and gym teachers are trying to teach children how to absorb the shock of falling. In tumbling, you learn to tuck and roll. If you consider falling off an act of tumbling at speed, then you should follow the same guidelines if you can. You'll probably want to analyze, calculate and make a fast decision as you're falling, and that can be a real downfall. Kids don't get hurt as often because they just tuck and roll instinctively without a lot of deliberation.

Rule number three, don't hold onto the reins. That's a good way to dislocate your shoulder, or give your horse such a yank in the mouth that he gets even more upset than he was when you and he went separate ways.

One of the most important aspects of parting company with your horse is the moment when the fall is finished. In most cases, there is a window of opportunity to get up quickly and get a hand on your horse. Usually, the horse is standing stunned for a few seconds, surprised that his rider is no longer with him. That's when you can grab him. If you miss that opportunity, the horse is probably going to leave the premises, and it's going to be a very long walk home for you. So we urge our riders not to dwell on the moment and lie there, assessing or analyzing. We tell them to get up quickly, but not in a way that startles the horse, and take hold of the reins for the safety of the animal. If he runs off, he could be hurt. You have to have it in your head during the act of falling, "I've got to catch my horse." Also, the odds are that the environment you fall off in is not safe for the horse without you. If it's in a ring, fine; but a cross-country course or the trails are a whole different story.

Naturally, should you be badly hurt, or terribly stunned, don't try to get up. If you're at an event, the first-aid crew will be there soon enough, and you don't want to make your injury worse.

It's also a good idea to carry a cell phone when you're riding outside the ring, so in the event of a fall you can call for help. Make sure your emergency numbers and the stable number are programmed into your phone. Carry the phone on your person, not on your saddle, because it will be useless to you if the horse runs off with it.

CHAPTER FIVE

Mom proffers carrots to my first horse, Midnight

Growing Up with Horses

I T WAS NO SURPRISE that I wound up working with horses for a living. Animals have always been a big part of my life. One reason they meant so much to me as a kid was because I felt quite shy; I couldn't even bring myself to say grace at large family dinners. While I was growing up, I always found animals easier to talk to than most people.

The first animal I had a close connection with was Sing Sing, our cat, but I enjoyed the same communication with horses. That connection developed further as I learned more about how they thought and fine-tuned my riding skills.

My riding career really started with my first horse, Midnight. He was my eleventh-birthday present, purchased for all of $600—a price that included his saddle and bridle. The people we bought him from lived just a few miles away; my father, Phil, simply drove over there and then rode him home to our 25-acre farm in Massachusetts.

Midnight and I did not have an immediate rapport, however. One of the first things I remember about this black gelding, who looked huge from my pre-teen vantage point, was riding him out on the lawn, where he promptly dropped his head to eat. Try as I might, I was too little to separate him from the grass, so he had a big snack that afternoon. (David had the same experience with his first pony. We both found out early—and not for the last time—that horses don't always do what you want them to do.)

Eventually, though, Midnight and I got along better, and riding became the highlight of my day. I would feed and muck in the morning before school. After classes, I'd hustle off the bus so I could be in the saddle by 3:30 p.m., and I usually didn't dismount until just before dark.

My involvement with horses meant I didn't participate in any after-school activities. Since I was a good athlete, it was almost frowned upon at school that I wasn't on the sports teams. People just didn't understand my so-called "horsing around." I remember many of my schoolmates and teachers saying, "When are you going to quit playing with your horses and play sports?"

What I couldn't explain to them was that riding was not just what I did; it was also becoming who I *was*. Giving my life to horses wasn't a decision; it was my only passion.

Fortunately, my parents and my grandmother, Angela, who lived with us, were totally supportive. So were my brothers, one older and one younger. Though they weren't riders, they also understood. And believe me, sometimes there was a lot to understand.

I'd seen jumping on TV. Great Britain's Princess Anne was competing in eventing, and I was following her career; she was one of my heroines, so I decided that was what I wanted to do, too. For my window of opportunity, I picked a day when my mother, Joanne, was going grocery shopping; I knew she'd be away for a few hours. We didn't own any jumps, of course, but I thought the kitchen furniture would do fine. I dragged it out on the lawn, setting up chairs as my jump standards, with brooms and sticks between them as my version of rails. The kitchen table, however, proved too big for me to attempt to clear—even when I turned it on its side. (Of course, I wasn't wearing a helmet or boots. I was in shorts and sneakers, because that's the way life was back then. While I miss the simplicity of that era—when kids simply rode and learned about horses, rather than specializing in a certain discipline—there's certainly a greater safety consciousness now, and that's a good thing.)

Anyway, there I was, leaping over the kitchen furniture aboard Midnight, when my mother came home early for some reason. She pulled up in the driveway, took it all in, and drew a couple of deep breaths. She didn't give me a hard time, but she did make an important decision: "I think," she told me, after we put the kitchen furniture back where it belonged, "that it's time for you to have some lessons."

So we joined the Groton Pony Club. We also found an instructor, a British woman by the name of Elizabeth Vickers, who was enormously helpful in teaching the whole family what three-day eventing was. The only time I'd heard the sport mentioned before that was when Elizabeth Taylor was on the Mike Douglas talk show. He said to her, "If you weren't an actress, what would you do?" She replied, "I probably would have been doing three-day-event horses, the kind of horses that Princess Anne rides." (Needless to say, that made me an Elizabeth Taylor fan. After all, she had been the heroine of *National Velvet*, a movie with which I could identify.)

Elizabeth Vickers told us that Midnight was not the proper horse for me, that I needed something smaller and more manageable. We sold him back to one of his former owners, and Elizabeth contacted Hideaway Farm in Geneseo, New York. The Harris family, who own it, have been breeding Connemaras for years. These animals, who trace their roots to Ireland, are sturdy, good-tempered, and generally fine jumpers. For me,

47

we purchased Erin's Shamrock, a distant relative of the famous Erin Go Bragh. At a different farm, we got another Connemara, named Moira, for my mother, so she and I could go out hacking together. (Though we called them "ponies," technically neither was actually pony size: Both stood a little more than 15 hands high, and ponies are 14.2 hands or under.)

Shamrock turned out to be perfect for eventing, which we got more involved in through Pony Club regional rallies and lessons with Elizabeth. He was really a dream horse; I was lucky to get such a talented animal so early in my riding endeavors.

I was also lucky to be living in a fortunate time and place for the development of eventing in this country. When I was twelve or thirteen, Neil Ayer—who went on to design the cross-country courses for the 1984 Olympics and 1986 World Championships and founded the organization now known as the US Eventing Association—began putting on the Ledyard Farm Horse Trials at his home in Massachusetts, not far from our farm. He brought over the biggest names in European eventing to compete. They included my idol, Princess Anne; Jane Holderness-Roddam; Lucinda Prior-Palmer; and Mark Phillips (who would go on to marry Princess Anne and one day be my coach on the US Equestrian Team).

Though I would get to know all of them well, at that time I was just a star-struck kid asking for their autographs. I was well-placed for that, right in the thick of things: This was before people began using two-way radios to transmit scores, so I volunteered to be a courier. Riding my pony, with a satchel slung over my shoulder, I would deposit the fence judges' score sheets in my bag, then ride Pony Express-style (but slower) to the chief scorer so everything could be tabulated.

When Neil eventually offered an Open Preliminary three-day event at Ledyard, I entered. Pam Fessenden, who was an A-rated Pony Clubber, helped me there. My dressage was getting pretty darn good; I was only fourteen and I won the dressage, against all the grown-up, full-time riders. (The dressage phase in eventing was rather elementary in those days.)

However, I must confess I really did not understand the whole steeplechase concept. I didn't know enough to wear a watch, so I had 10 or 15 time faults; that cost me the competition. I managed to go clean in cross-country and show jumping, though, which meant I ended up fifth or sixth.

The experience really was a hoot. "I have to do this again," I told everyone, though I don't think anyone—myself included—realized that I'd be doing it hundreds more times during the succeeding decades, all over the world.

By that point, I had changed instructors and become involved with Chick-A-Tee Farm in Pepperell, Massachusetts. Its owner, Austin Mason, was doing a lot of really great things on his farm with dressage, and I was now starting to get a lot of dressage lessons. He'd have masters like Nuño Oliviera from Portugal come with one of his instructors, Patricia Findley. Robert Hall came over from England, too, and he arranged for me to ride with one of his top students, William Micklem, whose family is very big in horses in England. William's brother, Charlie, worked for British World Champion Lucinda Prior-Palmer (now Lucinda Green). It was all starting to come together as I met more and more people who helped me become involved in the world of eventing.

My dad had his own foam-rubber business. He would always leave work to take Shamrock and me to Pony Club. It was a family project: Mom would pack a lunch, Dad would drive, and we'd all go together. I remember vividly getting my learner's permit when I turned sixteen. The next day I had a lesson with Robert Hall. It was a great moment, because Dad could stay at the office and I finally could drive the trailer while my mom kept an eye on me from the passenger seat.

During the summers, I would go down to Cape Cod and spend a month with hunter/jumper rider Julie Ulrich and her husband, Richard. I competed in the Medal and Maclay equitation classes there. I never qualified for the finals in either competition, because Erin's Shamrock was definitely an event pony, rather than a long-legged, smooth-striding equitation horse. But Julie worked on improving my style, and that was an important part of the foundation for my riding career.

Still, eventing continued to be my real focus. At that time, Pony Club was huge in New England; I did a lot of eventing with fellow Pony Clubber Mark Weissbecker, who would go on to ride with me on the USET. After camp with Julie on the Cape, I'd go to the Green Mountain Horse Association in Woodstock, Vermont, and do more camps there; I even took part in a GMHA 50-mile trail ride up that way. I was happy to do it all, because to me it was all *riding*.

One thing I stayed away from, though, was foxhunting—even though it's a sport that has been a springboard for so many eventers. I tried it, going out with the Myopia Hunt, but it scared me to death because Shamrock got so aggressive in the hunt field. It was all I could do to keep him from passing the Master of Foxhounds, which would have been a major no-no—especially since Neil Ayer was the MFH at that time. I remember thinking, "This is a little crazy." So I stopped hunting and did not take it up again until years later.

Just as I was beginning to make eventing my specialty, the USET moved its eventing operation to South Hamilton, Massachusetts. Soon things were really happening up there, making my "neighborhood" an even better place to be for a young eventing hopeful.

I was on the team for the first North American Young Riders Championship in 1974. It was at Joker's Hill in Ontario and it wasn't a particularly auspicious occasion; I fell on landing over a big oxer that had a drop to it. A lot of others did the same, but that was small comfort.

Still, I was playing the game, and these were important days for eventing. At the same time that the Young Riders was going, the 1974 World Championships were happening in England, half a world away. Beth Perkins competed there with a broken foot, and I remember thinking how extraordinary that was—in the days before I, too, would ride despite injuries because that was part of the game.

This was the World Championships at which Bruce Davidson became the first American to win the title. That win paved the way for the US to host the World Championships in 1978 for the first time, and that opportunity became the start of the Rolex Kentucky Three-Day Event, the country's biggest event. It eventually became one of only four annual events in the world that enjoy the highest-difficulty rating, four stars.

All that was far in the future, however, when in 1975, a year after the Worlds, I first hooked up for lessons with Tad Coffin. Tad, who had won the individual gold medal that summer at the Pan American Games, was in training with the USET, and he used to drive out to our place to teach me. He'd come back to the house and have dinner with us before returning to the team's South Hamilton training facility, so we'd hear all the inside stories about the eventing world.

In 1976, I finished second in the Young Riders Championship, less than a point behind first place. It was a landmark year: I'd turned eighteen and had just graduated from high school. We had a family conversation about college that lasted all of a half-hour. There was no question about the direction I was headed, and my mom and dad said they would support me 100 percent. But they warned that if the family was going to make the sacrifices of time and money to back me, I would have to give 110 percent effort. There would be no compromise on that.

Of course, I was delighted. But the way things turned out, my decision wouldn't be quite as simple as it appeared at that moment.

That summer of 1976 was remarkable for something else. Tad went to the Olympics in Montreal; he asked me to look after the horses he was training who weren't going to the Games. They were stabled at his parents' home in Strafford, Vermont, just a hop and a skip from Canada. Naturally, we wanted to go to the Games, so on cross-country day we got up really early, fed the horses, and headed north.

My first glimpse of the Olympics live, rather than on TV, was awe-inspiring and overwhelming, as I was planning what I wanted to do in the sport. However, it also emphasized how tough, and often heartbreaking, eventing can be. I saw Princess Anne fall in the water jump and World Champion Bruce Davidson do the same. So when Tad wound up with both the team gold medal and the individual gold on Bally Cor, I had even more respect for him. (I never imagined that, many years later, I would compete the only granddaughter of Bally Cor, the very courageous mare Bally Mar.)

After the Games, I followed Tad to a new barn, Flying Horse Farm, owned by John and Diane Pingree (who eventually would breed and own Bally Mar). But I soon found myself under more pressure than I could handle at eighteen. I had wanted to go to the Radnor Hunt three-day event for a shot at the new Harry T. Peters Trophy, which was *the* award for riders in my age group to win. But because I had been second, not first, at Young Riders, Tad decided to keep me home. He has a tremendous work ethic; he taught that if you're going to be at the top of this sport, you really have to work very hard—and you've got to get out there and practice and practice until you master whatever weakness you have in your riding. Unfortunately, his approach made me start doubting myself. My riding began to deteriorate, and my dressage tests were terrible.

At that point, I felt that I had to re-evaluate whether I was going to do this as my profession. I thought I had made that decision months earlier. Now, though, I found myself trying to figure out whether I thought of eventing as an enhancement of my life or as something that I was giving things up in the rest of my life to do—because if you feel you're giving things up to pursue an ambition, then it's probably not what you're meant to do. You'll wind up resenting the effort you put into it.

Also preying on my mind was a feeling that I was never going to be good enough—because the group above me was *so* good, and so young: Tad, Bruce, Mike Plumb, and Jimmy Wofford. It seemed as if there might never be a time for me. Am I ever going to make the team? Am I ever going to get to the Olympics? Who's going to knock those guys off the top? All I had were questions, and no answers.

My generation was people like my boyfriend at the time, Derek DiGrazia; Grant Schneidmann; Ralph Hill; and Bea Perkins. Karen Stives was in the dressage world during that period. She came on very quickly when she got into eventing, a few years later, but she was also Mike Plumb's girlfriend, so that helped fast-track her. Of course, we all did wind up riding internationally, and Karen and I eventually won several Olympic medals between us. At the time, though, I was plagued with doubts for all of us—but mostly for me.

In the winter, I finally left Tad's place and took a month off to go home, regroup, and try to figure out what I was going to do—in other words, if I was going to continue riding full-time. Again, I had huge family support; we talked about it a lot. For me, though, it was total panic. Sometimes I really did think maybe I should quit and go to school. After all, my parents had met at Boston University; my mom, who got a degree in architecture, was even valedictorian of her class.

But as it turned out, that was her road, not mine. I decided to stick with the riding. It became obvious, however, that I needed a change in both location and approach.

Bea Perkins, Beth's sister, was my best friend at the time, and she was a working student for Jimmy Wofford in Virginia, as was Derek. Destiny pointed me in that direction—except for one thing: Jimmy couldn't take me as a student! His barn was already full. I understood, but that made things difficult, because at the time he was one of only three people to choose from if I wanted a trainer after I left Tad. The others were Bruce and Mike—and neither was in Virginia, which was where I wanted to go.

Fortunately, Bea's mom, Essie, called Jimmy on my behalf and he relented: A couple of weeks later, he phoned to say he had shifted things around and made room for me. He was going to take me as a student after all. I was both relieved and nervous. I never really was able to express my appreciation to Essie for that phone call. It changed my life. Unfortunately, Essie's life was far too short as cancer got the best of her soon after that time. Still today, the US Eventing Association recognizes the leading lady event rider every year with a trophy in Essie's honor. Having won this award nine times has always been very special to me.

Naturally, Tad wasn't happy about my leaving his barn at first, and unfortunately we didn't speak for years after that. It made things very awkward when our paths crossed at competitions. However, the move was one that was very necessary for me at this point in my career. When you're trying to improve, you sometimes have to make hard decisions, as David and I have found over and over again. (Happily, even though I'm not on Tad's Christmas card list, we now have a mutual respect and some very good conversations whenever we run into each other.)

It's interesting that the only two Americans who have so far won the Olympic individual gold medal in eventing, Tad and David, have both so dramatically affected the path of my life. Tad, who later in life found his niche in the saddle business, helped shape my riding with lessons about rhythm and position and straightness of horses. He had very much the military, structured approach, which he learned from then-USET coach Jack Le Goff, who had been at France's famed cavalry academy at Saumur—and who taught the same lessons to David.

I went to Virginia on March 1, 1977. A new season of the year was about to start, along with a new season in my riding career.

Jimmy had a very different approach from Tad, and it took some time to get used to. On my first day with him, he simply sat on the arena fence and said, "Let me just watch you ride." He observed me for ten minutes, never saying a word.

Finally I couldn't stand the suspense any longer. "How does it look?" I asked him nervously.

"How does it feel?" he asked back.

Moments like that are branded in your memory. It's not about how it looks—it's about how it *feels*. If it feels as if you and the horse are together as one, it's going to look great.

But it didn't look great for quite a while, and things weren't easy once I started with Jimmy. I went through a stage of not being very successful—because, frankly, I wasn't riding very well. Between going through a change of instructors and adjusting to different styles of teaching, I'd hit a very low level of self-esteem. My highly competitive nature was a hurdle that I would have to overcome in order to recognize my weaknesses and improve on them.

Another factor was that Shamrock, my Connemara pony, had done so many things for me without my realizing it. When I began riding other horses, it became very obvious that I didn't know as much as I thought.

In spite of all that, I did get to the Advanced level that year, finishing fifth at Blue Ridge in the Advanced three-day. By then, though, I had done all I could with Shamrock. He was the perfect Intermediate horse, but going Advanced with him was stretching it. Also, he was getting older; and as the challenges increased, he had reached a level at which he was becoming uncomfortable.

Jimmy's recommendation was that we go to Ireland and buy me a horse with experience. And so we took off on my first trip to Europe—and the start of a whole new direction for my riding.

INSIGHT

Olympic Dreams

What child who rides seriously, or maybe even not so seriously, doesn't dream of being in the Olympic Games some day? There's no higher aspiration in horse sports than earning a medal against the best in the world. We're all reminded of it every four years with non-stop television coverage, but there are those of us who think about it every day. *(continued)*

If your youngster is one of those fantasizing about being on the podium before a crowd of thousands as the national anthem is played, don't offer discouraging words. Instead, use this as an opportunity to teach her or him some lessons about life and aspirations. All the people around that child, and none more important than her parents, have to allow her to dream. The dream can fuel motivation to be serious about a sport and to learn to achieve a goal. The child may never go to the Olympics—or get close—but the experience can be a lesson about trying to be the best in whatever you do, and how you go about the process.

The effort will help the child learn that life has to be about the journey, not the goal—and about finding a way to enjoy the journey, the frustrating parts along with the good moments, because they all become lessons in life. She needs to appreciate the responsibilities and still have fun, never losing sight of consideration for the horse while balancing the other demands that life makes, including schoolwork and chores around the house. It's valuable experience for the multi-tasking we are all called on to do these days in practically every walk of life.

There's a lot you can do to help the motivated young rider. If your child is really serious about going to the top of the sport, she has to surround herself with the best people in it. To help her do that, go to your local Pony Club. The people may live in your neighborhood, but they're part of a national organization whose graduates include many Olympians.

"Doing it right" with horses costs money, but you don't have to be rich to make a start. Let your child muck stalls, groom, or do whatever she has to do to earn lessons and hours in the saddle, or to pay board on a horse or pony. Many famous riders started that way, including eight-time American Grandprix Association Rider of the Year Margie Goldstein Engle. She hustled from the time she was a kid, doing stable chores for the privilege of riding, and wound up in the Olympics.

David and I have also worked very hard for what we have, and that experience has made our achievements all the sweeter. So we urge parents: Encourage your children to put forth their best effort and see how far they can go.

CHAPTER SIX

Being presented my Badminton ribbon by the Queen

March Brown

GOING TO IRELAND was magic. It was my first time ever abroad; my eyes were like saucers. Having Jimmy with me was lucky, because I didn't know anybody—and he knew everybody.

When we went to see March Brown, a beautiful Irish Thoroughbred, I was intimidated. This awesome horse was short-listed for the following year's 1978 World Championships at Kentucky with rider Jerry Sinnott—but in Ireland at that time, everything was for sale. This was a high-priced purchase, however: about $40,000, a major sum for a horse in those days. To afford it, my parents would have to take out a second mortgage. They did it, no questions asked; my grandmother, Angie, contributed, too. I was so lucky to have the support of my family. I hate to think where I'd be today without it—not to mention the fact that Mom and Dad still play major roles in our business.

At the time we got March Brown (whom we ended up calling "Roy" around the stable), I didn't think much about what would happen to Jerry when I bought his horse out from under him. It took me years to realize how much it had taken away from him; actually, the sale pretty much ended his career at the highest level. In retrospect, that's something I feel very badly about—but I also know that if we hadn't bought Roy, someone else probably would have.

I competed Roy through 1978 and did all right, though it was nothing to write home about. He was difficult in dressage but very, very good cross-country. Meanwhile, I was so young, and I thought everything was so simple: that if you did "this," you were going to get "that." Because Shamrock, my Connemara pony, had been so successful, I didn't realize what I didn't know. (By then I had said goodbye to my brave little partner. I leased him to several teenagers, and with them he went to the Young Rider championships for several years before he formally retired.)

That realization came down on me like a ton of bricks when I could no longer go out and win on the pony. Now I was faced with complicated horses, Thoroughbreds that were Ferraris—and I had no idea how to handle these equine sports cars. I was going through a treacherous, vulnerable period in my career, when things didn't happen the way they were planned. But at least by that time I didn't have any doubts that this was what I wanted to do.

The big problem, however, was that I also didn't always have a lot of confidence in my ability and my riding. Jimmy used to say a rider wears his confidence on his sleeve, but that you're only as good as your last performance. So it was easy for me to slip into a downward spiral competitively. And that experience taught me how you have to pick yourself up and dust yourself off and find the strength that will make it better—something I've had to do over and over in my career.

With March Brown, I was always good cross-country, but not as competitive as I had hoped. My parents never wondered (at least not in front of me) why they had gone into debt for him. They were encouraging, asking only (as always) that I give it my best; the rest was following the process and giving it time.

Jimmy had decided that he would compete with his star mount, Carawich, the next spring at Badminton. He targeted his advanced students at the time—Ann Hardaway, Wash Bishop, Karen Reuter, Derek DiGrazia, and me—to go with him. So in January 1979, we headed to our training base at the home of Lord and Lady Hugh Russell for a memorable experience. Lady Russell had suffered a fall hunting and was paralyzed from the waist down, so she'd gotten into driving. She's an incredibly good horsewoman, and you can still see her every year at Badminton, touring the course with her pony team pulling her carriage.

Both Ann Hardaway and I started indulging in British food, and I ballooned up to 140 pounds: about 20 more than I usually weigh. Jimmy was on my case about it, but I just kept having a good time—at least until I got to Badminton, the most famous three-day event in the world.

I didn't know much about Badminton, really, so I wasn't intimidated until I walked the course. Then I gulped and said, "What am I doing here?" For the first time in my life, a course had backed me up big time. As I remember it now, the ditches were gaping voids under huge log jumps, the lake was practically an ocean, and there were scary drops. I asked Jimmy, "Am I up to this job?"

He told me something I will always remember: "Where you would doubt your ability, remember you're sitting on one of the best horses in the world."

He was so right. March Brown was incredibly impressive and talented. (I'd love to have another crack at that horse, now that I have a bit better idea of what I'm doing.)

As awe-inspiring as being part of Badminton was, I needed to focus and buckle down for dressage. Back then, that phase was still relatively unimportant in the calculation of three-day-event scores, so I wasn't disappointed to be in the middle of the pack with my workmanlike but not stellar test. My real focus was cross-country.

By the time I got to the start box, rain was falling, which made the big course look even more ferocious. But I had my game face on and was determined to take a crack at it, even if we'd had hail or a snowstorm. I had learned from Jimmy that any time you see a jump that intimidates you, turn your intimidation into aggression to get it right, whether that means to steady or to kick on.

The course (it ran clockwise that year) was going fine until I almost fell off at the infamous Quarry, which came early in that year's configuration. I remember Roy pulling himself up next to the crowd at the rope. I shimmied back into the tack in my trademark fashion (as I quite often did after getting dislodged), managed to stay aboard, and—amazingly—was sixth after the cross-country.

The next day Roy was tired, and I didn't know how to ride a tired horse in the show jumping, so we ended up with four rails down. That dropped us from sixth to tenth. But my result was really great, because only fifteen finished out of forty starters. Completing Badminton was an achievement in itself. And, of course, it was the biggest accomplishment of my riding career thus far: completing a course that was significantly more difficult than anything I'd ever experienced. I'd never even dreamed of getting a ribbon—I was just there for the experience.

The top ten in the placings got a small silver trophy of a horse: a miniature replica of the actual Badminton trophy. Mine remains one of my most cherished competitive souvenirs, as is true for everyone who's been fortunate enough to earn one of "the little horses," as the British have nicknamed them. (David and I have six or seven of them between us—practically a herd—and we keep them all proudly on our mantelpiece.)

To top off my Badminton experience, Queen Elizabeth was presenting the ribbons! I was practically in a state of shock, but at least I knew enough to curtsy to her. She said to me, "I watched your horse on cross-country. I knew the horse a little when Jerry Sinnott rode him. He's lovely to watch cross-country." I was practically speechless; I could only think, "You watched my horse go?" What I managed to say, though, was a proper "Thank you, ma'am." (There are clear guidelines to follow in conversing with the royal family. You don't engage in idle chit-chat on such occasions. Even with Princess Anne, who has been such a big part of the eventing community and very generous to us, there is a certain protocol we must follow in addressing her; we can't be too familiar. She has a difficult role to fill, and I appreciate how I'm supposed to behave in that context.)

Badminton was a thrill, but it wasn't until I came home that what I'd accomplished really hit me. Mike Plumb came up to me and said, "You may not realize this now, but you will always look back on it and realize how big a deal being tenth at Badminton is." And it wasn't until then that I finally thought, "Darn, I shouldn't have had those four rails down."

Even so, I'd done well enough to help uphold the honor of our stable. Jimmy had finished fourth. Karen Reuter's horse was also tired on show-jumping day; she ended up getting eliminated for three refusals. Wash didn't finish, and Derek hadn't been able to start because of an injury to his horse. Ann Hardaway hadn't gone to Badminton after all; she wound up competing at the Windsor Castle horse trials two weeks later instead. So I guess I was the star pupil—for a while, anyway.

But, as Jimmy always says, you're only as good as your last performance—and, as I've found, no matter what I've achieved, things can change in a hurry. In eventing, it's a real quick trip from the heights to the depths, and I've had a lot of round-trip tickets.

After that first Badminton, for example, things went sour quickly. That autumn, on cross-country in the Ledyard Farm Horse Trials, I stood off and went for a long one at the imposing Weldon's Wall (named after Badminton course designer Frank Weldon). It was the wrong decision. Roy cracked his stifle on the fence, fracturing his patella in five pieces. Luckily, he didn't have to be put down, but he needed a year off to heal.

At the time, the young horses I had were injured, too. It was really discouraging: I'd had a ribbon at Badminton in the spring, but by that fall I had nothing. That, unfortunately, can be a pretty typical scenario in this sport.

Tired and discouraged, I told Jimmy I was going home to figure out what would happen next. He wouldn't hear of it. I'll never forget how he sat me down and said, "The one thing you're not going to do is go home—because if you do, it will be an unhealthy situation. You won't ride there, and you need to ride."

"What am I going to do?" I asked, totally lost.

His answer was typically Jimmy: "Get a job riding." He rang up a friend of his, Colonel John Russell, who was in San Antonio, Texas, and I moved down there to work for four or five months. (Fortunately, I had relatives in the area who put me up.)

Colonel Russell was training athletes for the modern pentathlon: an overall test of ability that involves running, swimming, shooting, fencing, and riding. It's an Olympic event, but at the time he was working toward a big international competition to be held at Fort Sam Houston.

The way pentathlon horses become eligible for such competitions is to have someone who is not a pentathlete qualify them by jumping a clean round over the same 4-foot course they'll face in the pentathlon. I was hired to be the person to qualify seventy horses, working with the colonel's son, Doug, who went on to be a professional jumper rider and trainer. We would ride from 6:00 to 10:00 a.m. every day; in those four hours, I would probably jump eight or nine horses. The horses were all donated, so some of them had some real baggage. A few were legitimate good jumpers; others were dealing with soundness or behavior issues.

Early on in my partnership with Erin Shamrock.

With my great buddy Ann Hardaway
(Taylor) at the 1978 World
Championships in Lexington.

Here I am later, and a bit more accomplished, with Erin Shamrock. We were second at Radnor in 1977.

Wilton Fair in the process of winning his final competition, Fair Hill, 1993.

With Mr. Maxwell, getting some dressage pointers from Lars Sederholm, coach of the US team at that time. Mr. Maxwell was as beautiful to work with as he was to look at.

Lende Time!

In the vet box at Fair Hill in 1993: I was so cold that day that, in between my cross-country rides on Prince Panache and Shannon, I went back to the hotel and took a hot shower!

With Tailor before one of many trot-ups. We are very proud of how immaculately turned out our horses are, thanks to the O'Connor staff.

© BRANT GAMMA

My former coach, Jimmy Wofford, congratulates me on my Rolex Kentucky win in 1995 with Tailor.

© BRANT GAMMA

Photographer Brant Gamma, a good friend of ours, made this photo of David, Jill, Bruce and me (note my thumb!) into a poster. I had given a copy to rider Will Faudree, with a note written on it saying that I fully expected to get a signed poster of him up on that podium one day. Will lost everything when his house and barn were struck by lightning in the summer of 2004 (fortunately, no horses were involved). When he was asked what of value he missed most, he named a painting his grandfather had given him—and this poster.

*With a young
Biko and Snickers
before our move
to England.*

One of many memorable celebrations post-Atlanta!

After Atlanta, in the receiving line at the White House with the Clintons: The team members had been instructed to go in separately, per protocol, but David and I had wanted to go in together. As we were being herded off across the room, the President looked up, gave us a big smile, and said, "Look, Hillary, it's the O'Connors!" So we ended up being allowed to go in together after all.

With Mark and Sandy Phillips, who have given us so much through their knowledge and expertise.

At home at Stonehall Farm with Tex and Nash, who are enjoying well-deserved retirements. Tex still does some demonstrations with David, and Nash is ridden daily by Jacquie Mars or her good friend Anne Cleland.

The O'Connor Event Team posed for our 1997 Christmas card: Behind us, left to right: Sue Clark, Worth The Trust, Anne Ferrio, Rattle 'N' Hum, Michelle Schipe, Night Rhythm, Amy Spatz, On A Mission, Coleen Hayduk, Giltedge, Alice Clapham, Lightfoot, Jodi Platto, Joker's Wild, Paul Goodness, Biko, Charlie Morgan, Custom Made, Kirstie Douglas, Kingfisher, Kent Allen, DVM, Prince Panache, Michelle Lawrence, Another Song, Joanne Lende, Leslie Clift.

My 1997 Rolex Kentucky victory gallop aboard Worth the Trust, owned by Joan Goswell.

Our great friends Dick and Vita Thompson, owners of wonderful horses including Castlewellan, Mr. Maxwell, Park Hall, Biko, Nos Ecus, Joker's Wild and Upstage.

For me, to jump so many horses a day was the most incredible experience. The intensity of the work had a great impact on my show jumping, fast-tracking my education in a phase of eventing that is becoming ever more important. I started to develop a better eye to a jump, to understand my balance and my horse's balance—things that would pay off in the long run in future events, where so many titles are decided by a single rail. And I got paid $100 a week to do it.

I stayed in San Antonio until January 1, 1980. Then I went back to Virginia and brought my horses back from Massachusetts, where they'd been while I was in Texas. Ann Hardaway and I decided we'd get a barn together and put our shingle out to see what we could do for some income.

Roy spent that winter at the Middleburg Equine Swim Center. We were trying to keep him in shape without putting stress on his legs, as working him on the ground would have done. (Back then we didn't have a whole lot of choices. Veterinary care was pretty primitive compared with what we have now in terms of diagnostic tools, therapy, and surgical options.)

Though Roy returned to competition, he never came back to the same level. He did Chesterland that autumn, when I fell and broke my collarbone—another downer. It was again time for a change.

I sold a horse into the show world, and that gave me a little money to spend on a replacement for Roy. I went back to Ireland and got in touch with my old friend William Micklem, who was coaching that country's Young Rider team. We went to Punchestown together, and he showed me a horse named Kilgrogan. He'd been a jumper, not an event horse, and he liked to run away with everybody—but he had possibilities (William thought I might be able to manage him), and the price was right: Because he was such a runaway, I got him for about $20,000, which was really cheap.

I took him home and, sure enough, he *was* a runaway. Nevertheless, he was a fantastic jumper, and I loved him. The next spring, 1981, we went to Kentucky, and he placed well there. So I got selected for the US team going to Luhmühlen, Germany, where the World Championships were going to be the next year.

This 1981 trip was a kind of dry run. I didn't do that well because my dressage was weak and that phase was beginning to have more of an influence. (The standard was changing because Mark Todd, who would go on and win two individual Olympic gold medals, had moved to England from New Zealand and was crafting a new level of excellence in the sport.) I was clear cross-country, though, which gave me (and my confidence) enough of a boost to finish in the top twenty.

I made the team for the 1982 World Championships—but we missed the trip when Kilgrogan colicked the night before we were to leave and we couldn't catch the flight.

I was devastated. Here was something I'd been working toward for years, and it was taken away from me at the last minute. Then things got worse: Kilgrogan contracted peritonitis. Luckily, he pulled out of it that summer.

Our next big moment together was going to the Rolex Kentucky event in 1983. Kilgrogan did well enough there to get us named to a USET squad that would be going on a European tour. But a week after Kentucky, he came in from turnout with a large swelling on his shoulder blade. It didn't go down, even after the vet lanced it. It started bleeding and wouldn't stop.

We took him up to the University of Pennsylvania's New Bolton Center and they did exploratory surgery on him. The news was bad; he had a tumor, called a hemangiosarcoma, behind his shoulder blade. It was inoperable and terminal.

The doctors at New Bolton wanted to keep Kilgrogan as an anatomical specimen, but I said no, I couldn't bear it. My horse meant more to me than that; I owed him some peace before he died. I brought him home and gave him two weeks of being out in the field with his buddies before we put him down.

I wasn't present for that. I couldn't stand to watch my wonderful horse's life end. Jimmy stood in for me, cautioning, "I'll do this for you, but you'll return the favor for me someday." (And I did: Some years later, when his favorite mount, Carawich, had to be put down, I stood in for him.)

After Kilgrogan's death, it was back to square one, which was beginning to be a familiar place. But then I had one of the greatest breaks of my riding career. A woman from Potomac, Maryland, called me; I think she got my name from Jimmy. (That is one of the great things about the guy best known around the eventing world as Wofford, or simply "Woff." He'd encouraged Ann and me to go out on our own—and he sent us work, because he was inundated with students.) Her hunt horses were in Virginia, and she had a rider by the name of Laura Tillbury working for her, getting them fit. Laura wanted to be an event rider, so I was asked if I could give her some lessons. Eventually she wanted to buy Laura an event horse that the two of them could do as a project together. I helped out there, too, finding them a nice bay Thoroughbred, Bristol Bay, that we called Rex.

The woman, whom I then knew only as Jacqueline Badger, was great to work for. When Laura left her employment to go back to school, Jacquie wanted me to sell Rex, which I did after competing him for a while. She then asked whether I'd like to take the money and buy another horse as a project for the two of us.

At that time, as our business had grown, Ann Hardaway and I had moved from a seven-stall barn to a twenty-stall barn at Interhorse, a Middleburg farm owned by Alejandro Orfila. Mr. Orfila, the Argentine ambassador to the US (he went on to be the secretary-general of the Organization of American States) had been given an Argentine horse named Rutilante, who liked to jump. That was out of his area of expertise—he had Peruvian Paso Finos and Andalusians. I was dating his son, Alex, at the time, so it all worked out: I asked Jacquie if she was interested, and we got together on Rutilante. I competed him up through Preliminary level, then sold him on as a Young Rider horse.

While my relationship with Jacquie continued to grow through the horses, it wasn't until the 1984 Olympics that I realized that her maiden name was Mars and she was the daughter of Forrest Mars, founder of the M&M/Mars confectionary company. The revelation came only when she invited me to come watch the Los Angeles Games. Both of Jacquie's parents were there also. It was a fantastic trip, and I felt very honored to be included.

Like my trip to the 1976 Olympics, being at the 1984 Games was an inspiration for me, particularly when the US won the team gold and Karen Stives took the individual silver. The next time I went to the Olympics, I decided, I wanted to do it as a rider.

Jimmy Wofford knew that was where I wanted to go, and he was helping me get there. Ann and I were still taking lessons from him; they weren't easy, because he expected a lot. He always told us, "If you want to make the Olympic team, don't ever give the selectors a reason not to take you." He also insisted that our horses had to be turned out beautifully for their lessons, and we had to wear clean breeches and boots every day.

I have high standards, too, and the lessons I've learned from people like Jimmy have helped me to meet my goals—because when you expect a lot, you have a better shot at getting it. But many of the things I expected to accomplish when I first went down to Virginia took a lot longer than I anticipated.

Handling the Death of a Horse

When a horse you have ridden for a long time dies, it's a loss in so many ways more than just the obvious sadness of parting with an old friend. You also lose the knowledge that only this horse had of you as a rider and partner—the result of a long and fruitful mutual respect. If the horse was one you have grown to love, one with whom you had experiences that you can't really explain to anybody, being without him can be a wrenching situation.

But if you are faced with the difficult situation of putting an old horse down, you have to think beyond the moment, beyond the sense of emptiness you feel as you recall your sacred times with this horse. In fact, if you hang on to a memory in the wrong way, it can be destructive to your relationship with your next horse.

So don't dwell on the experiences you had with your old horse so much that you close yourself off to the possibility of new experiences that can be just as fulfilling. Remember: If you could enjoy such special times with the horse who's gone, you have a gift of communication with these animals—a gift you can continue to share with other horses. You'll find that there is another horse for you somewhere, a horse you haven't even met yet, whose development will be a tribute to what you learned with your former horse. It's not unlike getting a new puppy after your old dog dies—but it's more intense, because the act of riding a horse adds another aspect to the relationship.

Another thing to remember is that the quality of a life is more important than the quantity of a life. That's how you deal with deciding to put a horse down. Waiting too long, just because you want to keep him around for your own sake, is irresponsible. You must act if he's not happy within himself, if he's not eating, or if he's having a hard time getting around. Don't put it off until he's stopped absorbing his food, his teeth are falling out, or he founders and can't walk. You won't want to wake up one morning and find that your horse died alone, out in the field, perhaps with a broken hip, because you weren't *(continued)* kind enough to send him to his rest earlier, with dignity and without pain.

Losing a horse suddenly, however, is a very different emotional experience. Truthfully, there is no preparation for a catastrophic event that is fatal. It hits you much harder than letting go of an older horse when you've come to realize it's appropriate to put him down.

The untimely death of a horse is not unlike the untimely death of a human. And when you're actually the one who was on board during a fatal accident, it's even worse. Some accidents are unavoidable; others occur through an error in judgment. If you're the person who ultimately caused the death of that horse, that's an aspect that weighs very heavily, taking a steep toll of guilt and remorse.

Even in this kind of case, though, you have to think about moving on and taking what you've learned to find another horse and make *his* life better. You have to pull yourself up by the bootstraps and remind yourself that you know how to care for a horse, and that there's a horse out there that needs caring for.

A death, any death, of someone close to you leaves a void. Try to fill it with other things. Trust us: There will always be a special place in your heart for every horse that gave you so much. Though his physical being may have left the earth, you will eternally cherish who he was and what he taught you.

CHAPTER SEVEN

Receiving instructions from Jimmy Wofford

Moving Up—and Down

I WAS AT the Green Mountain Horse Association Horse Trials in Vermont, after the Los Angeles Games in 1984, when Jimmy Wofford called.

"How would you like a nice Advanced horse to compete?" he asked. Not sure whether he was kidding, I replied cautiously, "Sure, that would be really nice. Do you have any ideas?"

He told me he was retiring, but his horse, owned by Mr. and Mrs. Richard Thompson, wasn't. "Castlewellan is twelve years old, and he's still 'on.' I talked to the Thompsons, and we thought you might be interested."

I was a little confused, so my first reaction was very mixed: "What? Aren't you going to continue riding him? You're Jimmy Wofford. This is what you do."

He explained that he really felt he needed a career change; he had done everything he wanted to do in competition, and this horse needed to carry on. So I said, "If that's really what you're going to do, I would love to take over the ride on Castlewellan."

That was, of course, an understatement. I couldn't believe my luck! I had loved Castlewellan before I ever even sat on him. And because I was at Jimmy's barn, I knew the horse we called Paddy really well.

As it turned out, we seemed to suit each other. Paddy was the first competition horse in my adult life that I found was a really nice complement to my lack of strength as a woman (as opposed to horses I'd had in the past who, frankly, were often a little strong for me). He was very successful already, and he became the first horse I had at the upper levels that I learned how to win on.

Paddy's best phase was definitely dressage. He had been brought on in England by Judy Bradwell, who is a lovely rider altogether and produces her young horses beautifully. He was a horse who would win dressage at Badminton and Burghley. His temperament during the test was beautiful; he never got nervous. And this was a perfect pairing, because I had a problem with dressage: I didn't like it. To me, it was a necessary evil to put up with because it was the way to get to the jumping phases. Paddy was the first horse on whom I could appreciate the essence of dressage: that it isn't about what you're doing in a 20-by-60-meter arena, but about the communication you have with your horse. He was a teacher and I was definitely a student, at least in that phase. Also, I really enjoyed him cross-country. He was an efficient galloper, very smart: careful and brave at the same time.

In show jumping, though, I feel that I helped him. He had a terrible drift to the right, and he became the first horse on whom I figured out how to correct a straightness problem in jumping. So we learned together.

My most memorable competition with Paddy was winning Chesterland in 1985. I was first in the dressage phase, and I remember to this day all three judges giving me perfect 10's on the medium-trot circle. I don't think I've ever ridden another horse with such an extravagant and balanced medium and extended trot as he had. Another reason why that Chesterland was memorable was that a hurricane swept in on cross-country day; we had to move the horses over to the Radnor Hunt Club, more than twenty miles away, because the tents we used for stabling at Chesterland weren't safe in the storm. Saturday was a washout, so we did cross-country on Sunday and stadium jumping on Monday.

I also had The Optimist there, and Lutin V. Lutin finished third, but we didn't get a ribbon because I had to ride him *hors du concours*—the rules didn't allow competitors to ride more than two horses.

The next year, the World Championships were in Gawler, Australia— and our preparations for that started in January, which made for a long winter. We needed to be in a northern climate for forty-five days, then had to go into isolation quarantine for thirty days because of Australia's strict quarantine rules. (Those rules had been eased a lot, though, since 1956, when the Olympics were in Melbourne but the equestrian events had to be held in Sweden because no nation's riders were willing to leave their horses in quarantine for six months!)

First we went to the USET headquarters in South Hamilton, Massachusetts, where we worked in the indoor arena. Then we headed south to the USET's main stable in Gladstone, New Jersey. All of us involved with the team were together for ten weeks, which was a real experience in itself: You learned how you wanted to act and also how you did *not* want to act. Being one of the young guys, so to speak, I just hung in there and kept my head down, taking in what it meant to be part of the USET.

At Gladstone, ten days before we were going to leave, Castlewellan got up from rolling and clocked the top of his hock on the cast-iron feed tub in his stall. His hock blew up; he was quite lame. So though he'd made the team, he wouldn't make the championships.

This was a situation that was becoming all too familiar to me: I'd qualify for a team; then something would go wrong with my horse. It was very frustrating—but I knew it was only as frustrating as I wanted to make it. To keep my perspective, I compared my situation with that of people who hadn't even gotten that far. And in fact I was fortunate in that I did wind up going to Australia—with Lutin, who was short-listed for the team and a wonderful back-up horse for Paddy. He was every bit as good; he just wasn't as far along in his experience.

This was my first trip Down Under, and I loved it. One of my fondest memories is of riding Lutin out in the bush and whistling, as I often do when I'm in a good mood. All of a sudden, my whistle came back at me. A beautiful cockatoo was sitting in a tree, imitating my little tune.

But though the setting was memorable, this World Championships wasn't the best of events for the US. As a team, we were eliminated; only Mike Plumb and I finished. And I had a cheap fall coming out of the water: I wasn't paying attention, and Lutin tripped while cantering up the step. We fell, and I separated my left shoulder—but was still able to put in a clear show-jumping round next day. (I didn't think about not competing on the final day. It's a reflex at that point; you never want to deny your horse a chance he deserves to complete a major competition.)

Mike finished eighth on his 1984 Olympic mount, Blue Stone. I ended up eighteenth; that trip up the step had cost me a silver medal. I had the right horse—a real cross-country machine—at the right moment in time to get done what I had trained so long to do, and I disappointed myself. But the Gawler experience gave me the desire to teach myself to concentrate more thoroughly on every aspect of what I do.

Lutin, my partner at Gawler, meant a lot to me because he'd been purchased for me as a token of appreciation by the Firestone family, who had entered my life in the summer of 1983. Jimmy Wofford had gotten a phone call from Bert Firestone, whose son, Matthew, was at the North American Young Riders Championship at Flying Horse Farm in Massachusetts. Matt had been training with Denny Emerson in Vermont;

Mr. Firestone wanted him to be closer to home in Waterford, Virginia. At the time, Jimmy was getting ready for the 1984 Olympic Games and was not taking on new students, so he suggested the Firestones call me instead. Matt came over with some horses he had bought in Ireland. That was how I met The Optimist: a very big, very strong, $7/8$ Thoroughbred who rode as big and strong as he looked—and Matt was a small guy. Naturally, he found it very difficult to keep this horse under control. At the Young Riders competition, The Optimist had run off on steeplechase; Matt had not been able to pull up, so he'd ended up doing another circuit of the steeplechase before he was able to stop his four-legged runaway train.

As I started to teach Matt, I realized that the size and strength of The Optimist were overwhelming for him. After watching him struggle with the horse for a few days, I thought, "This is not supposed to be this hard." I called Bert Firestone and said, "We need to find Matt a more suitable horse." He asked what could be done with The Optimist, and I said, "I'll be happy to help you sell him to someone who knows how to handle this type of horse." When he asked whether I could handle him, I said I could try, but I didn't promise anything.

That was my first experience with the Firestones as owners, and they proved to be terrific. In the autumn of 1984, they sent me to the Boekelo event in Holland with The Optimist, and he won it. The weather was in my favor: Torrential rain made the track deep and heavy, so the horse did not run off with me; I could actually let go of the reins and kick him. He logged the fastest time of the day in this trench of mud he had to gallop through for ten or eleven minutes. That gave us a pretty good lead going into show jumping—the first time I'd ever been ahead prior to that phase in a major competition.

My nerves got to The Optimist in the warm-up, where he stopped at a fence for the first time in his life; I almost fell off. But that broke the ice, and I relaxed. When he ended up winning, it was really great for everybody: I had won overseas for the first time, and The Optimist had proven what he could really do, fulfilling the promise he'd shown when we won Radnor the previous fall.

As it happened, I was not the only one to win a big prize with The Optimist. Two years later, recovering from my separated shoulder following Gawler, I asked Jimmy to come out of retirement and handle the horse at Kentucky, which he did. He won there—and to this day, people ask me about my riding "Jimmy's horse," The Optimist. On the other hand, people also ask *him* about his riding "Karen's horse," Castlewellan. When you win a big one on your home ground, the horse you're riding all of a sudden becomes "your" horse in the eyes of the public, even if it's only a borrowed ride.

Being involved with the Firestones, a horsey family who really trusted me to teach their son, was a great turning point in my life. It made me feel I had something to offer back. When you're trying to carve out your own career at that age, you're always doubting yourself. But the Firestones helped my self-confidence: They expected a high standard, and so often I was able to deliver it for them.

They also sent me over to Ireland with Matt to get him a more suitable horse—seven years after Jimmy Wofford had done the same for me. Unlike my situation, though, it wasn't Matt's first trip to Ireland—his family owned a lovely stud farm over there. We found Santex, who would end up taking Matt from Young Riders to four-star level, including making a USET squad for the alternate World Championships in Poland in 1986. Matt was quite a good athlete, and we struggled with the dressage together. Although he was very successful, I wish I could do it over again; teaching him with what I know today, I'd do a lot better. But isn't that always the way? I think you always try to teach better, find ways to improve communication, no matter how long you do it. It would be fun for me now to teach Matt at the age he was then. Back then, though, he was in his teens and I was in my twenties; considering that, I think we did a pretty good job together.

Before the Polish outing, I went to Burghley for the first time, finishing fifth on Lutin. But that side trip meant Matt and I took a different route to Poland from that of the other US competitors, including David and Bruce Davidson. They flew to West Germany, then went by truck to East Germany (this was still in the dangerous era of the Berlin Wall) and on to Poland. We flew from Heathrow in London to Warsaw, and from there to Poznan, Poland.

We arrived in Poznan at 9:00 p.m., on the last plane of the night. We were supposed to be met right outside the terminal by a driver. The arrangements had been made by a travel agency in Germany, through the USET. When we landed, the first thing we did was exchange our money from dollars to zlotys, the Polish currency. The travel agency had encouraged us to do this. What they didn't mention was that zlotys are not exchangeable for any other currency—and that you can't change them back to dollars. So we had pockets bulging with zlotys and very little left in the way of dollars. (Naturally, it would turn out that all the Poles wanted to trade in was dollars.)

By the time we got to the curb and realized there was no one waiting to meet us, all the lights in the airport had gone off. It was closed until morning. There were no cell phones in those days, and no way to call anybody. We didn't speak the language or know how to get where we were going. It was very scary; I had never felt so far away from home. My mind kept going back to the guard with the machine gun on our plane, who had barred access to the pilot's cabin so no one would hijack us to the West.

Standing in the dark, alone and frightened, we were lucky enough to find someone across the street who spoke broken English and gave us a lift to a hotel. After we got our rooms, I gave the hotel clerk the number for the travel agency in West Germany. He said, "We will ring you in your room to let you know when the phone call comes through."

"How long will that take?" I asked, desperate and trying not to show it, knowing that they were holding our passports at the desk.

"Normally, three days," said the desk clerk. My jaw dropped. "We have to have clearance to have you use the line," he said apologetically.

I told him we were riding in a Polish competition and needed to be there on time with the assistance of the travel agency we were trying to contact. He told us the fastest he could do it was midday the next day. And that was that.

We were stranded, unable to get in touch with Matt's parents or my parents. Here I was, acting as guardian to Bert's son, and I had him over there in the Eastern Bloc. No one knew where we were, and we didn't know how we could get ourselves to where we were expected to be. It was a nightmare worthy of a made-for-TV movie.

After some very long hours, we talked to a travel agent in Germany the next day. The agent got us a car and driver, and we started off to a training facility a couple of hours from Bialy Bor, the scene of the competition, where the Polish Young Riders' equestrian center was located. It was an interesting way to start the weekend.

After we got there, we found out that the trip hadn't just been crazy from our perspective. David had traveled in the horseboxes with everyone else, in a convoy driving through West Germany, East Germany, and into Poland. In the middle of the night, they got stopped by the army. We heard how the soldiers frisked Bruce Davidson (they were probably the only people ever who weren't intimidated by him!) after shining a flashlight in his eyes.

Not long after arriving, I developed dysentery from the water. I became pretty sick and wasn't sure if I could compete. Running every few minutes to the communal bathroom left me feeling weak and pondering what I had done to deserve this. (They had warned us not to drink the water, but I was pretty naive and thought that if I boiled the water, I could use it to brush my teeth. Wrong.) Thank goodness, Ginny Leng of the British team fixed me up with some type of charcoal medicine. The Brits had brought more human medicine than the US contingent did.

Aside from my having the runs, the event was really fun, though not without other hardships. It was held in a rural area in late summer, so the weather was getting cold. We were in cottages, with one women's shower and one men's shower, but no hot water for either. Brrrrrr. So much for the glamorous lifestyle of international eventing stars.

The competition went well, though. Our team finished second behind Britain. Individually, David was second, I was fourth (just out of the individual medals) on The Optimist, and Matt was tenth with Santex. We were so successful as a team that we got quite a lot of prize money—in zlotys. So we had all this cash. We used some of it to buy local crafts at the trade fair. The rest of it we gave to one of the Young Riders there, who had been nice to us. I don't know if that helped him; I can only hope so, because I never saw him again.

Poland was pretty grim in those days; I'd never been exposed to the realities of political oppression before. What amazed me was that, despite the conditions under which they existed, the Polish people turned out to be some of the nicest, most trusting folks I've ever met in my life. David and I became good friends on that trip. Dating-wise, we were both involved with other people at the time. But there was no question that we shared a lot of the same interests; we had fun just getting to know each other. Until then, our paths really hadn't crossed—except for that time at Rolex he's told you about, where he was all banged up. But he was seventeen then, and I was twenty-one: a big difference at that age. After that, he had gone to college and then lived up in Massachusetts, doing Area 1 events, while I was in Virginia and doing Area 2 events, so the twain never met.

Following Poland, we both found ourselves at the same invitational event in Jamaica—where I got dysentery for the second time. Aside from that, it was a wonderful trip; we got to be very good friends with all the British people who were there, including Ian Stark and Lorna Clarke, as well as Cathy Wieschhoff from the US. David and I grew closer there, too. Then we came home, back to our old lives.

I think we each decided over that winter that we needed to make a change. I had been with Alex Orfila for seven years, but the thought of marriage didn't seem to be on the horizon for either of us: probably a sign that it wasn't a forever thing. Meanwhile, everything about David attracted me. He's very smart and intellectual, and he loves animals and is kind to them—all the things that I admire. He always made me laugh. And he was strong enough for me. In any relationship that's going to last, you need mutual respect. We don't have to "stand up to" each other; we have a communication that solves these issues early on.

So our being together gradually came to seem natural and inevitable—though, like our eventing careers, our relationship had to go through some downs before we hit the up part that would take us on the path of lifetime commitment.

INSIGHT

The Bolter

The bolter is a horse that has anxiety about his job. These horses very rarely bolt just because they want to run. A Thoroughbred might be apt to bolt if he came from the racetrack, because racehorses have been taught to run when they are put in stressful environments. There are some ex-racehorses with enough confidence that they're not overcome by anxiety, but they're hard to find.

If you buy a bolter, you'll be dealing with the habit for the rest of his life. So think twice about buying one, especially if you're at a lower level of riding.

There are things you can do to curb a horse's tendency to bolt. For one, you can try to ease his anxiety about his job with careful training, never asking him to do something that is beyond his ability or his level of schooling.

The way you ride him will also help. You want to adjust your body language, finding a position that doesn't ask him to slow down or speed up. If he gets quick and nervous and you react by starting to pull while you're grabbing with your legs, you've pushed the "go button" and the "whoa button" at the same time. That will only increase his anxiety and exacerbate the bolting problem. So you need to find the power of neutral: having your body position independent and well-balanced, so you're not asking him to go faster or slower.

If you're struggling with this—and if you're physically capable—you could try to get a job galloping racehorses to practice dealing with speed. But make sure you're a very, very good rider before you even think of trying something like that.

But even if you're just working on your own to make your position more independent, you can get some of the same effect by shortening your stirrups to galloping length and trotting and cantering around the ring. The difference between the length of stirrup you use for dressage and for galloping is major, eight to ten holes. Even the difference between your show-jumping length and galloping length is significant and can be as much as three to four holes.

It's a lot of work, and you'll have sore muscles for a while, but it's the fastest way to get fit. Also, it teaches you balance—because you can't ride by grip. (When you first start practicing this, you might want to use a more experienced, steady horse until you have your balance down pat. Then try it on a horse you find more challenging.)

If you are involved with a bolter, you're going to have at least one time when he gets away from you. That calls for an emergency stop: Bend him with an opening rein and then use a direct rein. Getting this to work requires preparation, though. Before you have to deal with a runaway situation, you need to teach him what you want when you bend him to a stop. Start practicing the technique at the walk: Bend him with one rein, gradually bringing that elbow to and behind your hip. Keep bringing it back until he finds his balance and is under control. Don't use your leg or an outside rein to balance him, and you'll find he learns to come to a halt easily.

CHAPTER EIGHT

© BRANT GAMMA

In the dressage arena with Wilbur

Visiting England

IN SEPTEMBER 1987, I took Border Raider to Burghley, one of two annual events in the world at that time that were rated at four stars (the other was its spring companion, Badminton.) Border Raider had a problem with ditches and walls, and I ended up in the middle of Centaur's Leap, but I was still the only American who finished. Karen had had a nasty fall with Lutin V. I was scheduled to ride after her, and I went ahead on course.

We had discussed this eventuality and decided that if one of us fell, the other would try to carry on. Given all the variables that make a trip happen, and thinking about the horses' chances and the owners' expense, we realized it would not be prudent for either of us to bail out just to visit the hospital and see if the other one was OK. This agreement has become something we've had lots of practice applying, most recently at Fair Hill in 2003, when I broke my wrist and ankle in a cross-country fall and Karen went on to win the three-star CCI and place second in the Pan American Championships—just as I was coming out of the recovery room following my operation.

Back at Burghley in 1987, though, Karen had a much more serious injury. She was bleeding from her left kidney and had sustained a broken pelvis and ribs. The fall had happened over the RM fence (named for then-sponsor Remy Martin), which is shaped like those letters. She was long to the first corner, which made her even longer to the second corner. That didn't put her in a good spot for the bounce fence that followed. Lutin hit the vertical on the way up with both knees, and she got caught in the crossfire between the horse and the fence. She told me that her last thought before hitting the ground was "This is going to hurt." What really did the damage was that Lutin knelt on her torso as he struggled to keep his balance.

After Burghley (which New Zealander Mark Todd won, riding Wilton Fair), I stayed with Karen for thirty-six hours, until she was transferred to another hospital. The one to which she'd been taken right after her fall was a gritty public-health facility—where her standard of care got a big upgrade after Mark Phillips came to visit. At the time, he was still married to Princess Anne, and everyone on the staff knew who he was. Once he left, the nurses were all over Karen, wondering if the Princess Royal might drop by. "Hmmm. Anything's possible," she told them, and got another round of coddling.

As soon as I knew Karen was in good hands (her mom, Joanne, stayed with her for two or three weeks), I went home, because she had asked me to ride one of her horses, Talk Of The Town, at Chesterland. On the plane returning to the US, I met a man named David Lenaburg, who introduced himself by saying he had seen me ride at Burghley. We had a lively conversation. After we got back to the States, he called and asked me to find a horse for him. Then the insurance company he owned sponsored me for a while. But most important, he's been a great mentor and friend for what's now a seventeen-year-relationship. (This little story just goes to show that you never know when or how you're going to meet up with someone or something that will end up being influential in your life.)

Things, meanwhile, were looking up. Talk Of The Town and I won the Preliminary division at Chesterland. Then I was approached by Bert Firestone and his wife, Diana, the owners of the Kentucky Derby-winning mare Genuine Risk—and of Lutin, the horse Karen had ridden at Burghley. They wanted me to go to England to look at horses with their son, Matt (whom Karen had worked with, of course). The trip would have the added benefit of enabling us to pick up Karen on the way home. She was barely well enough to travel, and would be much more able to do so safely on a private plane, accompanied by friends to help her.

Matt and I flew over on the Firestones' Falcon 50 and landed at an airport in Peterborough, near the hospital. Then we went down to visit with Mark Todd and look at Wilton Fair, his Burghley winner. It was a productive trip: We bought Wilton Fair for Matt, swooped up Karen, and flew home.

But, Wilton Fair—nicknamed Wilbur—turned out to be just too big and strong for Matt. So the next year, 1988, the Firestones sent him to Karen to sell. When nobody wanted to buy him, she asked me to ride him, figuring that because I was bigger and stronger than she was, Wilbur and I might get along well. I liked him. And, luckily, David Lenaburg had seen him win at Burghley and relished the idea of owning the horse. That turned out to be a fantastic break for me.

However, I flipped him in our first competition together, at Rocking Horse in Florida in the beginning of 1989: He was jumping up onto a bridge, and his feet slipped under a rail. By the time we went to Kentucky that spring, he'd started having a tendon problem as a result of the Florida fall, so he got the rest of that year off.

That problem was just one example of how this sport can discourage you in so many ways, but I've learned not to give up. And in this case, persistence really paid off: Wilbur went on to become one of my most memorable mounts.

At the 1990 edition of Rolex Kentucky, I knew we could be competitive in the dressage, and that worked fine: We finished in first place, just a whisker in front of seven-time Olympian Mike Plumb on Chagall. But the next day we had to go cross-country in a torrential downpour so intense that I needed to pull out of the short route for one combination I was jumping because I couldn't see it behind the curtain of rain; I went the long way instead. Things got so bad that they stopped the next horse after me, putting a hold on course until the rain subsided.

We were still in the lead going into stadium jumping. I just had to hold it together—something that became even more of a challenge when Mike was fault-free. Wilbur and I were able to do the same, though, securing victory at America's most prestigious event. This was a real landmark in my career as I successfully coped with what we came to call "Wilbur weather."

Wilbur taught me that I could come out on top at the three-star level. It was an important mental boost after winning a bunch of one-stars and two-stars, though I still hadn't made it on the true international circuit. After all, I'd only been an alternate with Take The Rapids for the 1988 Olympics: In that year's selection trials, held in Kentucky (and a test so difficult that I called it a five-star, even though there's officially no such thing), Take The Rapids was putting in a tremendous trip until it all went wrong when he caught a hind leg on the double corners at the end of the course and had a fall. I didn't make the team.

I had a difficult time dealing with my disappointment, because I'd felt I had a good shot at the Games. I went to Seoul anyway, to help Karen. But despite this show of support, it was a stressful time in our relationship—she had made the team and I hadn't. We actually split up for six months the next year—mostly, I think, because I was too young to deal with my failure.

Still, my disappointment made me determined not to miss out on the next big international opportunity, and my 1990 victory at Rolex got me on the team for the first World Equestrian Games, to be held in Sweden that summer. The WEG was supposed to be a one-time experiment, putting the World Championships in every FEI discipline in the same place. It was organized so well in Stockholm, however, that it became a permanent fixture on the competition scene. That is how our eventing World Championships are still held, halfway through every four-year Olympic cycle. The 2006 WEG is in Aachen, Germany, and we're hoping that the Kentucky Horse Park—home of Rolex Kentucky—will get it in 2010.

But that first WEG, exciting as the concept was, turned out disappointing in many ways for me. Though I did well enough in dressage, there was a very difficult bank combination on cross-country that was not riding well in the way we US riders all had planned it under our coach, Lars Sederholm, a Swede who was living in England. He tried to tell me about another way to do it, but I didn't really understand—I guess because of a language barrier. When I came around the corner to line it up, it did not make sense to me; I got in really wrong, and Wilbur stopped.

The next day, in show jumping, I wound up with a good round to be eighteenth overall, but I came home without a medal either for myself or the team. It was frustrating and not at all the way I wanted to end my first appearance on the US team in an international championship.

INSIGHT

Communicating with Horses

When you're working with horses, two decisions take priority. First, from the moment you begin interacting with a horse, you must choose your line of direction. Second, you must decide how you get there. You can't just wander aimlessly; you need a plan. That's true whether you're thinking about jumping a course or how you will train the horse.

As you go on this journey, be aware that you take on a daunting responsibility as a rider: You are the custodian of the horse's trust, honesty, integrity, and dignity. You must respect the horse and make sure he has everything in his life that he needs.

History has too many examples of horses' trust and dignity being taken away by force. Thankfully, we live in a more enlightened age, where people are learning that you don't *force* horses to do anything. Instead, you *communicate* what you want. And, because horses are such genuine souls, they pretty much want to do it for you.

Our life with horses as a couple is far more enhanced than it would have been as individuals because we have been able to enjoy our journey and our horses together. Learning to enjoy the moment is part of the journey, and each moment goes by very fast. We really like helping others learn how to understand and appreciate their horses the way we do. When we teach our camps, people are with their horses seven hours a day. Being with them so much, either sitting in the saddle or holding them at the end of a line, gives them opportunities to gain new insights into the character of animals they may have owned for years.

Most people don't spend enough time with their horses to understand them properly. Take a lesson from the Native Americans, who just sit quietly in the pasture and study their horses. Try doing the same thing; watch how your horse behaves. You'll learn about his personality and how he thinks. You'll see his social interaction with other horses, and the way he reacts to a new stimulus. All this information will be very helpful as you train him.

Studying your horse while he is in the pasture, away from your influence, will make you much more aware of his personality type. Try this experiment: If you have four horses in a field and put a bucket of feed out there with them, typically you'll find that one horse goes right to it, two of the others run around complaining but not getting anything done, and one stands off in a corner, waiting for everyone else to be finished. He's submissive, but he's not a whiner like the two who are running around.

If you have a "bucket" horse—if yours is the one who eats first—you may have your hands full. You need to be a leader when you're dealing with him. If you're not a natural-born leader, *he'll* try to be the leader; you'll have a relationship that's much harder to deal with than the ideal situation.

When you're looking to buy a horse, ask the people selling him whether he's a follower or a leader. That will help you tune into what kind of personality he has. And be honest about assessing your own personality as you try to find a match that's compatible for you. If you're not honest with and about yourself, your horse will *make* you honest— probably the hard way.

CHAPTER NINE

© KARL LECK

Competing with The Optimist in the 1988 Olympics

Seoul Survivor

MAKING A LIVING with horses isn't easy. When I took stock of things at the end of 1986, I felt that I was at a point where I *could* support myself by working with the horses, but it was a financial struggle. I was never as pennywise as I should have been; I always wanted the best equipment for the horses in my barn but was afraid to charge their owners for it.

That whole time period in my twenties was a real roller coaster. When I sold a horse, I felt like I could pay all my bills. Then three months later I was back in the rut again. The fact is that horses are expensive; no revelation there, huh? But I often kept them too long and didn't have time to train and ride them properly, because I was off competing other horses, so the sales thing didn't always work.

A solution to my financial woes came along when I started doing clinics: an idea I got from Jimmy. I found that I was invited back time and again to the places I had given my first clinics. Soon I realized the clinics were the way I could keep costs down for the horse owners in my barn and enable myself to pay the bills.

Meanwhile, my big goal—like David's and that of nearly everyone— was, as I've told you before, to be in the Olympics. That was an important reason I'd stayed in the game, with all its hardships and heartbreaks.

My chance came in 1988, when the team was headed for Seoul, South Korea, though I never envisioned it turning out the way it did. Olympic dreams usually include medals and "The Star-Spangled Banner" playing before thousands of applauding spectators in a big stadium. But my Olympic debut, in a very foreign country, was a nightmare.

We quarantined at Chesterland during a hot summer of hard footing, coping with forty-five days of Pennsylvania heat that soared past 90 degrees. We never even did a horse trial before the Games. The last time our team horses had run cross-country was at Rolex Kentucky in April, and Seoul was in September.

Five of us short-listed riders—Phyllis Dawson and myself, David, Ann Hardaway, and Jane Sleeper—were pretty much following the guidance of discussions between *chef d'équipe* Mike Page and the sixth rider, Bruce Davidson, whose home base was Chesterland. Both were Olympic veterans, and Bruce didn't want to go cross-country before the Games because the ground was so unyielding.

I had been the alternate, but I moved up to a team position when both of Jane Sleeper's horses went lame. David remained an alternate; he came along to Seoul to give me moral support and get his first taste of the Olympics.

Unfortunately, the decision not to do any cross-country in the run-up to the Games didn't turn out to be the right answer for all of us— because we went out on that course in Korea and really felt rusty. Only two US riders finished: Phyllis, who came in tenth on Albany, and Bruce, who was eighteenth with Dr. Peaches.

When we got to Seoul, our horses—who hadn't competed for more than five months—were awfully strong. I remember taking The Optimist for a gallop around the track in Korea and being unable to stop him when he got up a head of steam. He came to a halt only after he ran into a line of Port-a-Johns—which wavered with the force of the blow as I heaved a sigh of relief that nothing worse had happened to us.

He did the same type of thing to me on the hilly cross-country course at Wondang Ranch. I reacted by riding very defensively, very "backwards," which proved to be my undoing. At the fourth fence, a vertical on a steep downhill, I went off. He just kept cantering down the galloping lane, prolonging my agony in front of the crowd, until I finally got ahead of him and caught him. I remounted, but when we got to the sixteenth fence, a very wide birch oxer on top of a hill, I put him in the middle of it twice and ended up eliminated. I had been fighting to stay in the game, but The Optimist apparently thought the oxer was a bounce, and I couldn't do anything to dissuade him.

Walking off the course on foot, I was totally dispirited. So much for the Olympics: The dream that had kept me fueled with desire to succeed through all the bad times had turned out to be the worst time of all.

I waited until later to cry. I wasn't sent there to bomb out, but it was hard to imagine how my first Olympics could have gone worse. I was really, really down—a mood that didn't lift as I flew home with David. Mike Page had told him, "Maybe we should have brought your horse." Maybe they should have.

At that point, I was an unhappy person. I had put my whole life into my Olympic effort, and look where it got me. Naturally, I was re-examining everything I did in light of the Games. Meanwhile, David was coming at it from a completely different angle, which was "Hey, you got to participate, and I didn't."

We were two strong personalities who were not happy with ourselves, let alone each other. It was only a few months afterward that, as David has told you, we split up, and we stayed apart for six months.

That was a very testing time, but we knew pretty quickly that we were meant to be together. Neither of us could get the other out of our minds. We were in the same town and doing the same competitions, so we'd see each other. It was very hard, and we were very bitter. Usually, we didn't even say hello.

By the autumn of 1989, we were both over it. We weren't married, we didn't have kids, and so we didn't have any reason to resume our relationship—other than the fact that we *wanted* to be together. And that was the best reason of all.

Though painful, being apart was a great exercise for us. Among other things, it made us realize that this career we both had chosen was going to have big highs and great lows. From that point on, we've never let the highs get so high that we couldn't take the lows. It's not that the highs aren't really exciting, or that the lows don't get us down. We just know we have to keep moving on to the next thing. That philosophy has kept us grounded in all the years since.

Handling Competition Jitters

Everybody has competition jitters. We do, too. The fact that you've been around the world and ridden in its biggest championships doesn't mean you're immune to that queasy feeling as the moment of truth gets closer.

So the question becomes, how do you deal with the jitters? You have to find your own methods of handling these nerves that make themselves felt before you ride into the dressage arena, show-jumping ring or out on a cross-country course.

First, ask yourself what you're afraid of. Are you worried that you're going to forget your dressage test? OK, then spend extra time memorizing it, and take a final look at a printed version just to reassure yourself before heading for the in-gate.

Are you afraid you can't jump the triple combination or make a left-hand turn to a liverpool? Then maybe your basics aren't good enough. Don't compete at such a high level that you're uneasy about the challenges it presents. Get yourself confident at the lower level; take a step up when you've got that nailed. You need to be solid in what you're doing before you try to compete.

Next, figure out what kind of pre-competition mood you prefer. Some people like to have a lot of support around them; others want to be more on their own. If you're just starting out competing, try both until you find your own routine. Then follow it so you always feel comfortable.

Relaxation exercises are important. Before you get on your horse, stop for a minute and consciously relax your body, piece by piece, from the top of your head to your feet. That technique also helps put you in a zone of concentration that eases the tension, so your first interaction with your horse before you're being judged happens in a relaxed way. You can also play music on a Walkman to prepare for your time in the spotlight. Try soothing classical music if you're really riled up; it will help calm you down. On the other hand, maybe you need   *(continued)*

93

to be pumped up; choose a favorite rock tune to invigorate you and shake out the cobwebs. Want to be inspired? How about the theme from the film *Chariots of Fire*?

Wearing a Walkman has another benefit. It can isolate you from the public (we're happy to give autographs, but don't ask us twenty minutes before our dressage time!) or from friends who might interrupt your train of thought as you're in the midst of preparing for your competition. That can get you off-track and break your concentration as you're visualizing yourself going around a course, so it's often good to have the Walkman bubble to protect you from intrusion. People are generally more hesitant to walk up to you if you have the earphones on. Just don't forget to take them off before you go in the ring!

Another key element is to start planning how you will spend the hours and minutes before you go in the ring. Following a pattern like that every time you compete gives you something familiar to hang onto, which automatically helps in quieting those shaking hands. And you won't have to wonder what to do next as the clock ticks down; you'll know how best to proceed, because you've done it before—and it worked.

A word of warning: Once you've established your routine, altering it drastically can cause havoc for you and your mount. Horses are creatures of habit; so if you make a last-minute change in the way you've always warmed up for the show jumping, for instance, you may raise problems you don't have time to fix. That could have a real impact on what happens in the ring. But you must also be flexible. If you suddenly run into bad weather, or poor footing in the warm-up area, don't be afraid to make whatever adjustments are necessary within the overall framework of your usual warm-up.

Develop a program and stick to it. You'll soon find that you're in control, not your flip-flopping stomach.

CHAPTER TEN

Biko, the US Eventing Association's Horse of the Century

A Change of Fortune

I N THE AUTUMN OF 1989, the Fair Hill International three-star
made its debut in Maryland. It was an auspicious one for me, because
I won aboard Nos Ecus, who belonged to Dick and Vita Thompson,
the lovely couple who also owned Castlewellan.

When I took over the Thompsons' horses, I kept them on the same
program and in the same place as they had been with Jimmy. And I kept
on their groom, Suzanne Schardien, who had gone to the Olympics and
World Championships with Jimmy. (Grooms are everything where horses
are concerned. They're as crucial to your team as a pit crew is to a
NASCAR driver. Our grooms are very, very dear to us. We don't even like
to call them "grooms," because to some people that sounds derogatory.
They're really our assistants—or, to put it more accurately, our horses' personal assistants. We generally refer to them as "staff.") Suzanne's presence

gave the horses real continuity. The Thompsons liked that kind of stability for their animals.

Nos Ecus had come from France, on the recommendation of Jack Le Goff. He was a pretty sharp little horse, but very flamboyant in his movement. He was plagued with soundness problems that we probably could have solved in this high-tech era, but that meant he didn't make it to the first World Equestrian Games in Stockholm in 1990, when David was on the team with Wilton Fair.

I went over to Sweden anyway, to support David, and it worked out a lot better than when he'd come along to Seoul while I was on the Olympic team two years earlier. We had grown a lot, and we'd learned how to root for each other.

Also in 1990, Matt Firestone bought a horse named Mr. Maxwell out of the stable yard of Con Power, an Irish jumper rider. Mr. Maxwell was another sharp little horse, but too complex for Matt's level at that time. (Being successful with one horse at a particular moment doesn't always mean you can handle other horses at that level—not unless you've had an upbringing where, right from ground zero, you've gotten tremendous experience with all types of horses.)

Max was also one of those horses who didn't have enough confidence for himself and his rider. This kind of horse can unravel very quickly, and so it was with Max. Matt had a bad fall with him in the winter at Rocking Horse Ranch: Mr. Maxwell overjumped coming out of a sunken road and Matt fell; then the horse ran over him.

Matt got hurt pretty seriously, and the experience proved to be a turning point: He decided that he didn't want to keep going down this road. He'd always had an entrepreneurial/investment side of his life that he was excited about, and this turned out to be the moment for him to take that on.

It was a turning point for me, too: As my relationship deepened with the Thompsons, who became very close to my parents, my work with the

Firestones was ending, though their friendship will always be dear to me. Their horses, The Optimist and Lutin, had retired. Their daughter, Alison, was not involved in eventing; she was embarking on a grand prix show-jumping career. And Matt, who had married and was moving to Florida, asked me to sell Mr. Maxwell.

Before I could do that, though, I'd have to get the horse's confidence back. Fortunately, the transition turned out to be easier than I expected. Max came along pretty quickly, the Thompsons wound up buying him for me—and he didn't take long to prove that he was a wise purchase.

Max placed well at Radnor in the fall of 1990, then won Kentucky the next spring. Five months later, he placed third at Burghley.

At that point, I moved my horses over to England, including a six-year-old named Biko who had done the Essex Horse Trials in New Jersey during the spring and was pretty impressive at the Preliminary level.

My good friend, William Micklem—who's probably had as much impact on my life as anybody else—had found Biko in Wexford, Ireland. He bought the horse and sold a share to Ronnie Duke from Northern Ireland. Not long afterward, on a buying spree in England and Ireland, Vita Thompson, my mother, and I stopped at the Dukes' "yard" (as the British and Irish call their stables). And the minute Vita saw Biko's big white blaze, she was sold on him.

"He looks like Nosy (Nos Ecus). I want to buy him; I want to buy him right now," she said.

I tried to counsel patience: "But you haven't even seen him go yet."

"I don't care. We don't need to see him go. He's beautiful. Let's buy him," she replied, a victim of love at first sight.

I convinced her not to say anything yet about her infatuation, warning, "If you do, the price might go up."

Then we watched him go—and he was, indeed, fantastic. I must admit I was also infatuated by this big, strong horse who was only five and just broken. So we bought him, for a lot of money—more than we'd ever paid for a young horse at that time. He turned out to be well worth it.

Still, Biko took some sorting out before he could start reaching his potential. He was a bit scared of people, because he hadn't interacted with them much. I'd say two years passed before I could get on him by myself, without people holding him. Gosh, I wish I knew then what I know now—but we did well enough together anyway.

Biko was the largest horse, but he could also turn himself into the smallest horse: He had such flexibility in the small of his back and the articulation of his stride that he could add a stride or leave one out without turning a hair. He had the grace of a ballerina and the strength of a giant, along with the eye of an eagle, the greatest heart, and elegance. There wasn't anything he couldn't do; he was a hero, and everything I always dreamed of in a horse. You could whisper to him on cross-country and get the job done. Truthfully, though, he was always too big for me. I think he might have been even more successful with a bigger person aboard who'd have more strength, power, and ability to transfer his balance and do it more quickly. I think David would have enjoyed that idea, too.

By 1992, I was feeling very well set. It was an important year, with the Olympics in Barcelona on the horizon. I felt sure I had a good chance at that, which was doubly important because I wanted to redeem myself on the Olympic front after the disaster of the 1988 Games. Nos Ecus was making a comeback, and Max was going great. The team was going to be chosen objectively: strictly on points earned in competition. The most points were going to be earned by the people who did well at the four-star events. At that time, there were still only two, Badminton and Burghley in England. (Kentucky and Adelaide in Australia both later became four-stars.) So what looked like the best strategy for me was to go to Badminton, rather than to a three-star; it seemed like a perfect progression from my wonderful placing at Burghley the previous year.

Unfortunately, it wasn't perfect. In fact, it was quite the opposite. We had treacherous rains that whole Badminton weekend. I even thought about not running. *Everyone* thought about not running, it was so bad out there. But I made the decision to run, and it's one I still regret.

The footing was very deep and wet. Spectators had ruined the take-off areas at the jumps by walking in front of them. (At that time, they had *carte blanche* to wander the course however they wanted to before the horses set out, and hundreds of thousands of human feet had done a number on the ground. Today, spectators are not allowed to walk in front of the jumps when they scope out a course.) By the time cross-country started, the area inside the ropes where we were running was just like Hershey's syrup: slick, chocolatey goo.

Trouble came early in the day. Olympic gold medalist Mark Todd had a crashing fall at the Vicar's Ditch obstacle with Face The Music, who broke a leg and had to be destroyed. The officials subsequently pulled that jump from the course and made everybody do what had been the long option there, which involved going across a bridge and jumping a gate at the end of the bridge. The very next fence was the infamous Vicarage Vee, another ditch.

I knew I was in trouble when they pulled the Vicar's Ditch, because Mr. Maxwell was really, really frightened of bridges. He was the kind of horse who would tremble when you got him on a bridge. But as much of a competitor as he was, I thought maybe I could get him across the bridge on sheer adrenaline.

We couldn't canter across the bridge because it was too narrow, with no railing. As soon as I got him on it, he kind of stopped to a walk, which meant I couldn't jump the 3-foot 7-inch gate at the end of it. So I had to take him off the bridge and re-approach the gate—and, for the first time ever, I had to hit him to get him across the bridge.

I'd already had one stop, and I had to think about whether I wanted to pull up and just call it a day. But I also was thinking about making it to the Barcelona Olympics, and the objective criteria that would get me there if I could just finish the course. Because I'd already gone about halfway around the course, I wouldn't have been able to do another three-day event that spring. These competitions are just too strenuous for a horse to be able to handle two of them in a short period of time. "What do you want to do?" I asked myself as time ticked away—and with it my hopes of making the Olympic team.

I decided to stay in and work on getting as quick a time as I could to avoid adding more penalties to the 20 faults I already had for the refusal at the gate. Though I was able to clear that fence on the second attempt, I also felt that Mr. Maxwell's confidence had been a little bit compromised because he'd been so worried about crossing that narrow bridge.

When I came to the Vicarage Vee, I thought I was on the right line to clear it, but Max jumped ever so slightly left on takeoff. He cleared the obstacle with three of his legs, but his left front foot just slipped on a piece of wood on the edge of the ditch. The wood was so wet that his foot skidded off there and he wound up face-first in the ditch, smacking his head and neck on the side of it. Max managed to get up out of the ditch, but it was obvious he was badly injured. His neck, which was in a contorted position, bulged ominously, and he was walking sideways.

Sick with apprehension, I loaded him in a horse trailer that had been driven up to where we stood, and we sped back to the stabling area. The vets X-rayed his neck and found that the first and second vertebrae were fractured. But we already knew what the ending would be, because he was convulsing.

I thought over and over again, "Why didn't I withdraw?" To this day, it's a question I still ask myself. Max had completely trusted me, and this was how it ended. Our only alternative was to put him down, because there was nothing the veterinarians could do for him.

The tragedy of Badminton 1992 didn't end with Max. William Fox-

Pitt, a very accomplished British rider, was aboard Briarlands Pippin when that horse lost a shoe and slid into the lake, breaking his back. It was one of the most awful days in the history of eventing, shaking the sport and prompting a well-deserved inquiry.

David, who wound up finishing seventh on Wilton Fair, was a wonderful support for me: there when I needed him, and very protective. That was something for which I was so grateful.

This was the first time I ever had a horse die out from under me, and it was very tough. My initial reaction was that I wanted to quit competing, quit the sport. "Why should I go on?" I wondered, totally miserable and blaming myself for the death of my wonderful partner. There was no question that I was completely responsible for this accident. I was the one who had put Mr. Maxwell on that fatal line at the Vicarage Vee. Yet he was the one who paid the ultimate price.

Badminton 1992 haunted me. The other two times when a horse has died with me in competition, I've relived that awful day with Mr. Maxwell. But the reason that I was able to carry on in the end was that I finally put it in my head in a place where I could deal with it.

I thought about the many horses that I hadn't met yet. If you give up, if you bail out on a situation you've given your life to, you're not giving yourself a chance. You're also not giving those horses, the ones you don't even know yet, a chance that you might improve their lives.

INSIGHT

Risk Taking and Winning

In eventing, getting hurt is always a possibility. There are times when that possibility gets into the forefront of your mind, and times when it doesn't. You can't dwell on it; you just have to keep going, putting one foot in front of the other. (If we feel unsafe while riding, we'll pull up. That happens every once in a while, always on some horse that's not "getting it.")

To some degree, by the time you reach the point where we are in our careers, you feel as if you've earned the right not to sit on a horse that is going to try to hurt you. You've met hundreds of them just like that one before, and you know what athleticism you have to use to make up that difference. As you get older, it's hard to draw on that well all the time. And as you get older, making the time isn't as easy as it used to be. You tend to start preparing for the jump earlier, slowing down too soon, and that all takes time. You're not as keen to go cross-country on a horse lacking in the appropriate level of communication.

In fact, as you get further up the levels, it's just flat out harder to win these events. Not only does your horse have to be sharp, but you require great technique to go fast enough to make the time. And behind that is all the preparation needed to have a good, solid, safe, and easy round for the horse.

We've always been the riders who wanted to maximize our technique and have the safe round. For us, the element of making the time is the last thing we consider, though I wouldn't say that's true of all event riders. There are riders who go for the clock first and get the technique over time. Their trips may be clear, but they're scary to watch.

We've tried to minimize the risks as much as possible, but there *are* risks in this sport. Still, we don't think of ourselves as risk-takers. We've never asked ourselves whether it's "worth the risk." This is what we do, this is what we like doing, and our horses like doing this as well. So instead we ask ourselves, "Has the risk become acceptably minimized?"

Because of the way we ride, we'll know when it's time to retire from doing the big cross-country courses. The signal will be a lack of speed and competitiveness. We'll find we're consistently ending up with 10 to 15 time faults and dropping from the top five, to the top twenty. At this point in our careers, though, we're as fast as we've ever been around a course.

We used to go fast at horse trials, to practice winning. But we've changed our focus at horse trials, because we don't need to practice winning as much; we've done it a lot. Now we save the speed for the three-day events; they're the ones we want to win.

Someone once asked us if winning eventually gets boring. Never. It's still about doing a good job. If you do a good job all the way around, you're going to win. Winning represents more than a trophy. It's the tremendous satisfaction for a job well done.

Some wins mean more than others, of course. When David won Fair Hill with The Native in 2001, that was a really cool moment and an emotional win because of who that horse was. He'd been sent to us four and a half years before that, to be sold, but no one else wanted to buy him; we ended up buying him, with Jacquie Mars. Though he had a tremendous jump, he was a difficult-minded horse, so it took a long time to get him to believe in what he did. The effort turned out to be worthwhile.

The Native's personality changed a lot as he trained. We didn't know if he would ever win a three-day event, or be "one of your famous horses," but he was one of the horses David enjoyed being around the most.

CHAPTER ELEVEN

© BRANT GAMMA

Karen and I are joined by her parents, Phil and Joanne Lende, niece Sarah Lende, and grandmother Angie

Coming Together

IN 1991, I went to Badminton with Wilbur—and found I had a cheering section. The group of people I'd been teaching at clinics in Utah had flown over to watch. Unfortunately, what they saw didn't give them much to applaud.

Wilbur came out of the starting box quite strong. At the third fence, he left on a long stride and jumped into the middle of the Huntsman's Close. After that, it only got worse. I had no way to put it together, and we kept missing.

There was just one thing for me to do at that point. I pulled up halfway through the course—the only time I've ever done so, but safety and common sense demanded it. Pulling up was devastating, though, because this was my first Badminton, which means it's one I'll always remember.

Things started looking up, however, when Lars Sederholm, with whom I had worked at the 1990 World Equestrian Games, came over and said, "Would you be interested in staying here in England? You can stay with me and do some riding for me. You're really talented; you're just going through a bad time."

My friends from Utah thought it would be a good thing. Lizzie Atkins, who had just sold her business, said, "I'm going to give you some money—I'm going to give you this amount this year, some the next year, and some the year after that. I don't care what you do with it. If you decide to stay here, stay; or go home if you want. But I think you should stay."

So, twenty-four hours later, I left Wilbur in England and went home to sell everything. I got out of my lease; sold the cars, furniture, and tack; and moved. England was where I spent the next four and a half years, and those years abroad were a big factor in making me the eventer I became.

Going to work with Jack Le Goff, which had been another quick decision, had changed my life nearly ten years before. This was the same type of thing: one of those situations where the door is open and you go through it or you walk away from it. And if I had been the type to walk away from opportunity, I wouldn't be where I am now.

There was one problem I faced in going to England: Karen and I had gotten back together as a couple, and she didn't know if she could move to Great Britain. When she came over for that fall's Burghley, though, she and Mark Phillips were able to put together an arrangement that enabled her to stay.

Mark, who was not yet coaching the US team, leased her space at Gatcombe Park, Princess Anne's beautiful estate. Though he and the Princess were divorcing, they were still legally married, and Mark continued to live at Gatcombe. The Princess graciously agreed to allow Karen to base herself there. (Jimmy Wofford is very close friends with Mark and the Princess. While the two of them were still together, they had vacationed at the Woffords' house while Karen was working there, so she'd gotten to know them a bit.)

Luckily, Karen's many owners (she had more than I did) were willing to support their horses in England instead of in the States. You've got to go where the action is when you're trying to improve yourself in a sport, and at that time the action was in England. There were many more events than in the US, most in close proximity, so we had countless opportunities to train and raise the level of our game.

Karen and I were based seventy minutes apart. I'd get over to Gatcombe once or twice a week, and she'd come to see me once or twice a week. In between those times, I was plenty busy. David Lenaburg decided to send over a horse named Night Rhythm, and Lizzie and her group sent On A Mission. We pointed him for the 1996 Olympics, and we sold clothes—T-shirts, sweatshirts, that kind of thing—to support the project. There were a lot of well-dressed people wearing On a Mission's clothes—but, unfortunately, he didn't make the Games. We had plenty of clothing left over, though, so we just crossed out the '96 and made it "2000" for Sydney. And when I won the gold medal, we got some new clothing with the logo "Mission Accomplished." It was wonderful to see creative people coming together to help me, folks like Beth Lendrum, who had been such a big part of the clothing effort.

My life in England wasn't the high life—I didn't have the money for it—but I got by. Lizzie's grant gave me $15,000 a year. Lars and I had a deal because I was teaching at his Waterstock Farm: I lived at his house for free and was treated like part of the family. Of course, I had practically no discretionary income, but somehow I managed to buy a car anyway, for 700 pounds (about $1100), that enabled me to get to Karen and to the lessons I gave "off campus." I also was sort of a commuter—by plane, not by car—to the US, coming back often to teach clinics. That turned out to be a good thing, because it kept a business going for me in the States.

There was a time, however, that I considered simply staying in Britain, where there was no question we could have remained and done well. I'm glad we didn't, though. As good as it was, it's not home—and that's something that's got to be number one when you're pondering what to do with the rest of your life.

Still, I wouldn't trade my experience in England for anything. It was crucial in my development as a rider and a teacher. At Waterstock, I was really in what amounted to a university setting, where I got to study people and horses. (Lars is very much a thinker and an experimenter.) That's where I was introduced to the round pen and the idea of doing loose work. The round pen is just what it sounds like: a big, fenced-in circle. It has no corners to hide in, so a horse can't get away from you there, which makes it a wonderful training device.

Another thing that helped was the atmosphere in the eventing community in England. In the US, up through the 1980s, anyone who got to the Advanced level expected to get on a team, and everyone was always worried that someone else was going to take their slot. It was constant tension. In England at the same time, there were people from many different countries competing; if you were from New Zealand and I was from America, I wasn't going to take your team slot, and vice versa, because we were representing different countries. That made things more collegial— and in that situation you have a true sport.

Now the same thing's happened here, although in a slightly different way. First of all, we have people who are competing at Advanced level who know they're *not* going to make a team. Maybe they don't even have any ambition to make a team; they just want to test themselves and their horses at the highest level. And the eventing scene on this continent is more international than it used to be: Canada's getting stronger, and we have Olympic team gold medalist Phillip Dutton from Australia and other people from elsewhere living here. Phillip and I, for instance, will go after each other competitively at an event, but at the end of the day we'll sit down, have a beer, and relax together.

This has made the sport much healthier, with more of a sporting attitude than there used to be. In the late 1980s, the US was just coming out of the Jack Le Goff era of pitting people against people to raise the competitive edge, which made riders angry at each other. Jack was successful in the medal count, but at high cost. That attitude was still strong when Karen and I left; when we came back, it had really changed, and suddenly *we* were influencing the *next* generation. Lars was a transition person for the USET: between the Le Goff era, the chaos and lack of leadership that followed, and the achievements of the years since Mark Phillips has been coaching the team.

In many ways, Lars was misunderstood on the US scene. I thought his greatest contribution to American eventing was to get people thinking about horsemanship, and to tune in our country to what the rest of the world was doing. The problem was that he tried to do a lot of it from England, and he's not the best communicator, so that didn't work very well. Still, it set up things and facilitated people's change of attitude to a less cutthroat, more generous approach.

I don't think Mark Phillips would have been so successful early on in his role as US coach if Lars hadn't helped in the transition. Mark would have had to spend two or three years laying the groundwork before he could have achieved anything with our program, I believe, if Lars hadn't paved the way.

While all this was going on, Karen and I were in the right places at the right times. It worked out really well: We had been in England during the change; then we returned and got a chance to make our mark when people were more open to our approach. One thing we thought was important involved bringing back the things we had learned about competitiveness and sportsmanship. I like to believe we helped put a sense of camaraderie back into the USET's eventing efforts.

One of the bonuses of being involved with eventing in England is its association with royalty. Princess Anne has always been very nice to us, making us feel a part of things on the social front as well as the sporting scene. For instance, I remember one night she invited us out to a pub for a bowling match, with the Gatcombe crew going up against the racing crew. This type of bowling is a game that was invented in 1300, a bit different from the high-tech version we're used to, but we all had a blast, including the Princess. She's a fantastic person to be around, though you couldn't pay me to do her job; her responsibilities are incredible.

She was our hostess for the Royal Military Review at the Wembley Arena, watching the armed forces doing drills and fun competitions. We had high tea in her apartment in Buckingham Palace that day. Police motorcycles blocked traffic for us, and our little bus didn't stop until it reached the gates of the palace. That's one of the perks of being with royalty: no sitting in traffic jams.

Princess Anne is very personable, very horse-related, and she's comfortable chatting with you if you're an eventer. After all, she knows plenty about the sport, having been the European champion and a member of Britain's 1976 Olympic team. Her second husband, Rear Admiral Timothy Laurence, is a very low-key guy. I took him to the Safeway supermarket when he was visiting Washington once, and he fit right in.

Despite all the benefits of being in England, we decided it was time to go home in 1994, when one of Karen's key horse owners, Jacquie Mars, asked us to come back to Virginia and run her place for her. Because we still had business in the US—we had clients there and gave clinics regularly—the transition was easy.

Truthfully, though, we were not the same Karen and David who originally moved to England. We came back different people, at a different level of riding, and with some different horses. For instance, I had Abigail Lufkin's very experienced Lighter Than Air, as well as On A Mission, so I returned with a new level of confidence.

Another difference: Karen and I found that our relationship had broadened and deepened while we were in England. Here's how it works: We're not two people trying to be the same person. Karen likes the contact on the phone and the office stuff, which I don't like. So there's a balance. I think we complement each other in many other ways, too. I tend to get into my shell; she likes to entertain. I'm much more of a planner than she is. And as Karen has helped me with my competitive side, I've helped her with her planning side.

Karen wins because she's competitive and athletic and her instinctive reactions are so quick. On the other hand, very few people call me a good cross-country rider. I'm not a risk-taker; I don't like it to go wrong. I'm not an artist like Mark Todd and Bruce Davidson. Someone once said the ideal situation is for David O'Connor to train and Mark Todd to ride. My horses win because of their training more than by any magic I work on the day of cross-country.

It's great to have two eventers in the family because we enjoy so much in common, but we don't coach each other unless the other person asks. I think a lot of equestrian couples make a mistake in the way they handle their marriages: In many cases, one is very dominant and the other ends up being a little bit of a student. Happily, we have worked at not going down that road.

I respect Karen for how she does our sport. It's a little different (though I have to say our approaches are more alike than they used to be). I always feel that "I don't need to totally do it your way; you don't need to totally do it my way; but if you want help, I'm here," and the same thing the other way around. If the other person is doing something you don't like, just walk away. (Both of us have done that.) What you don't ever want to do is say "I told you so." That's a bad thing for any marriage, and one you really have to avoid in the competitive world because emotions are so high.

The hard part of being in the same sport (as we found out at the 1988 Olympics) is when one person does really well and the other does not. You have to allow the other person to go through whatever they're going to go through. That's part of the healing process. You're there to support but you have to let them go through it. Don't try to change it. (Sometimes "hands off" is the hardest advice to follow.)

In 1992, after we had been talking seriously for six months or so about getting married, we decided to go ahead. Even though we had been together most of the time since 1986, it took us so long to get around to marriage because we needed to figure out how to make our businesses and our competitive natures work together. It came down to a discussion during dinner one night about whether we were ready to be together for the rest of our lives. I said romantically, "When do you want to do it?" Karen paused and said in her usual direct way but with a little smile, "Do what? Are you proposing to me?"

I ignored her and just said again, "When do you want to do it?" We always knew we were going to get married; it was timing, more than anything else, that was a problem. We contacted both sets of parents, and the news started slipping out.

At Loughanmore, a two-star event in Ireland a few weeks later, British eventer Karen Dixon stood up on a chair at the competitors' party, clinked her knife on a glass to get silence, and then announced, "What better place to celebrate the engagement of David O'Connor and Karen Lende?"

People asked how I had proposed, and Karen told them, "He really didn't." Our close friend, Swedish rider Anna Hermann, said, "David darling, you must get down on your knee and propose." So I did.

But when I asked Karen to marry me in front of everyone there, she wanted to be a wise guy and said, "I'll think about it." So I was a wise guy, too, turning around and asking Anna Hermann for *her* hand. She said yes. We got a good laugh out of that, and Karen decided she'd better say yes.

Karen and I got married in 1993, coming back to America only for the two weeks we needed for the wedding ceremony and surrounding festivities. It's different when your parents don't marry you off: This was *our* wedding, and *our* people. We're very close in eventing, like family, so of course we wanted everyone at the wedding. (Because we're in a little bit of a risk sport, I think we tend to share more in our friendships.)

Everyone had a party for us before the wedding, leading up to the big day. The ceremony was to take place on the porch of one of those stately Virginia mansions that are in the public trust. It was located fairly near our farm, in Long Branch, an area where Karen used to rent a stable. Time was pressing, as always; we were getting married on a Saturday and I'd be leaving Sunday night for Europe. Not much of a honeymoon. But we had a great time.

As you've probably figured out by now, our wedding was huge. We had 350 guests, people from New Zealand and Australia—from all over the world, really. Vicki Latta from the New Zealand team was there, and Mark Phillips, and Jacquie Mars, and so many of our other owners—including Joe Zada, who owns Custom Made.

We were to be married at 6:00 p.m. by Rev. Jack Filler, the Congregational minister who baptized Karen. He had served in the Korean War, and vowed that if he got out alive, he would devote his life to God. His first ministerial duty was burying Karen's grandfather, Peter Stevens, in 1957. His last was putting Karen's grandmother, Angie, to rest 47 years later. He obviously has quite a history with the Lende family. In fact, his son, James, is an eventer who came to us as a working student. Now James runs the riding program at Averett College in Virginia. Like everyone else who attended the wedding, the minister and his wife, Lee, found they had to wait for the ceremony.

There was a gatehouse a mile from the big house, and we had arranged for carriages to take us to the ceremony. We were getting ready to go when a big thunderstorm rolled in. That presented major trouble, since we had a tent without sides for the reception. (Why no sides? We couldn't afford them!) We wound up turning tables on their sides to block the rain.

It was pouring as wedding time drew closer, but the party already was in full swing, with the bar open and the band starting. Eventers don't like waiting for a celebration.

Karen and I were in touch by two-way radio, it being bad luck for the groom to see the bride before the ceremony and all that. She asked whether I wanted to wait and have the ceremony outside or just go ahead and hold it under the tent. I polled the guests, and they said, "We want to wait." Of course they did—everyone was drinking our liquor and busy having a great time.

Then I got another call from Karen, this time an urgent plea: "Please send champagne over to the gatehouse." She'd already been dressed, but she and her bridesmaids got out of their gowns during the delay—they didn't want them to get wrinkled. So they were having a little party of their own, in their underwear, while the bigger bash went on in the tent.

Meanwhile, Jacquie Mars had found the horses that were supposed to be pulling our carriages—in a trailer stuck on the side of a road. The truck that was pulling them had a flat tire; it was doubtful that they would make the wedding. Resourceful as always, Jacquie unhitched the truck, hitched up her Suburban to the trailer, and drove the horses to the wedding.

Finally the weather broke and the rain stopped. No one could be sure how long that welcome sunshine would last; we had to move fast and say our "I do's" before it poured again. But we found ourselves, as usual, waiting on Karen. She tends to be late, no matter what (except for her dressage tests). We have this great picture of Karen walking up the aisle as Brian and I are looking at our watches and shaking our heads.

At the end, after we were pronounced man and wife, an enormous rainbow appeared. It was like a special blessing of our union. And when people talked about the whole thing, they didn't call it "Karen and David's wedding"; they called it "The Wedding." It was a great time.

It Seems Like Only Yesterday*

by Phil Lende

It seems like only yesterday!
When the Lendes were young and a family
There was Karen and her brothers Steven and Chip
Life was full of fun, a wonderful trip.

It seems like only yesterday!
That David and Brian began their stay
There were birthdays and Xmas and school and such
Through the years Sally and Jay loved their boys very much.

It seems that horses were always there
Devoted to their sport were this handsome brotherly pair
It wasn't always "peaches and cream"
In the beginning, like everything, it was merely a dream.

And it seems like only yesterday!

Karen had to wait until she was eleven
While other kids rode when they were only seven
Her first was Midnight, big, black and of towering frame
She knew this packer could bring instant fame.

David and Brian with their mother made the trio
On horseback to the west. It seemed quite unreal
It was an experience for mom and her boys
From the east coast to the west coast ... they rode this country
and lived its joys.

And it seems like only yesterday!

And then there was Karen, oh we all remember it well.
She and Shamrock were competing, and they sometimes fell.
Once on her horse a big tree hit her head
They came back OK, but it is things like this we forever dread.

(continued)

115

David, too, had some bones that did not bend
His shoulder was one that took a while to mend
And there was his other shoulder, and a third shoulder too
His ribs took a beating and sometimes his body felt like glue.

And it seems like only yesterday!

Each went their course in an effort to excel
And excel they did, and they did it very well
First one made the team then the other did too
Riding as Americans for the red, white, and blue.

While competing in Poland, Dan Cupid placed his arrow
He shot his dart both straight and narrow
Right to their hearts did the love bug bite
Right from the start Cupid knew he was right.

And it seems like only yesterday!

Things have gone well for both our lovers
Thanks to their owners, their fathers and mothers
There is more ahead, more to see, more to do
Chapters yet to write, things to hear and see through

We are here today to celebrate
David and Karen on their wedding date
Joanne and Phil, Sally and Jay
We four are very happy, what more can we say?

As time goes on, what will we see?
Perhaps they will start their own family
And then in years we will hear them say
"It seems like only yesterday."

June 26, 1993

*Karen's father, Phil Lende, loves to write poetry for important occasions.
This is the piece he produced for Karen and David's wedding.*

CHAPTER TWELVE

Gathering for a team picture in Virginia

The O'Connor Event Team

ONCE WE WERE officially together as a couple, we had to combine everything. That's how "Team O'Connor" got started. All our various owners, horses, staff, and pieces of equipment were going to be part of one enterprise—and that took some doing.

We'd been a couple for seven years before we got married. One of the reasons why we dated so long involved wrestling with how to bring two very anchored support groups together as one support team. A big step in that direction was both symbolic and practical: combining our separate stable colors. David's were royal blue and black; mine were navy blue and light blue. So we ended up with navy blue and gray. (If you go into the archives of our equipment, you can still find some things in our old colors.)

117

It wasn't so easy to combine the people, not all of whom readily accepted the concept. Naturally, owners can be fiercely competitive; they didn't immediately start rooting for both David and me. We had to earn that, in terms of their believing this was a decision for life. You can see why they might be skeptical; people break up all the time.

We didn't have the option of being self-supported; in order to pursue our passion, we had to find a way to make it work financially. But beyond that, the team concept brought all kinds of benefits we never expected, from the unity and sense of camaraderie, to being able to call on so many people's intellects in our efforts. We learned that the only way to make people want to join our team is to have them believe in what we do. That was a conscious decision: to build something together that people would believe in and feel a part of. David Lenaburg became our first corporate sponsor with Bannerlife, and others followed.

And by the way, there was no question that I would change my name to O'Connor when I finally did get married. I'm pretty traditional in that regard. When I was growing up, women generally took their husbands' last names as their own. Period. So what I would be called after I married David amounted to a ten-second decision, which I actually had made some twenty years before.

The genesis of Team O'Connor may have been a dinner conversation long ago with a group of British riders who had relatives as their supporters. We knew that the most successful event competitors had one thing in common: a very solid support team, usually composed of mainly family members. So, we realized, why should we split our effort into separate camps when we actually could double our effort? Teams can be even more of an anchor because you're combining forces, rather than dividing.

One of the most important things about establishing Team O'Connor was to ensure we'd have multiple horses with which to go into the selection processes for the Olympics or World Championships. It became a brand that people recognized: something whose importance we'd picked up from the success of the "Mission '96" effort. We also knew we had to become more accessible to the public; we made a conscious decision to become public personalities. And the more we did, the more we realized that, as a sport, eventing was bad at marketing itself. Certainly competitors as a group had never given much thought to marketing the discipline as a sport to the general public. So we made sure we were always available for photo ops, to sign autographs and to reach out to the fans—who, after all, are vital to any sport.

Team O'Connor soon took on its own identity, and a big part of that has been our staff and all the people with whom we work. If you're creating a team, you don't just hire people to do a job; you have to inspire them intellectually to help get the group to whatever the goal is.

The scores of grooms that have become an intregal part of the OCET have had a profound effect on our successes. These unsung heroes take such incredible loving care of horses. I don't think we could ever thank them enough for their devotion.

One of the greatest additions to our team came when we moved back to the US. Jacquie had told us about a woman named Sue Clark who was her stable manager at her property in New Jersey. She wanted Sue to move down to the property in Virginia and continue the same position at Stonehall Farm. Sue willingly moved, lock, stock and barrel, and became not only stable manager but overall project manager. Her expertise in so many areas has helped us grow over the past decade. She does all of the planning on our trips abroad, all of the planning for our trip to Florida every year and, as a personal aside, has become my closest friend or, as we sometimes say, the sister I never had. David and I are truly grateful for her dedication to our program.

There are other key members of the O'Connor Event Team, like our blacksmith, Paul Goodness. His intellect is priceless. That's the key—not the hammer in his hand, but rather, getting his head involved. We have conversations with Paul about every horse every time they're shod. It's the same thing with our vets, Dr. Kent Allen and his partner, Dr. Christiana Ober, who've solved so many challenges for us.

We like giving credit to all these people. And when we started talking in public about how everyone worked together on our team, other competitors began to catch on. Now we hear of other teams out there, too. They don't all work the same, but any successful team needs to make sure that all the people involved—especially new staffers—understand its inner workings. For example, when I tell you that every year we have to get forty horses ready to ship to Florida for the winter, and pack all the equipment necessary to that move, you can understand how important our team model is to doing it successfully and arriving at the destination with all the horses and equipment we started with.

The team spirit has many manifestations. When David fell with Dunston Celtic on cross-country day at Fair Hill in 2003, breaking his ankle and wrist, one of his students was surprised to see me at the ten-minute box to help her shortly thereafter. She said that was when the concept of Team O'Connor really hit her. Even if I'd had to go to the hospital with David, I wouldn't have left her on her own: I would have talked to her on her cell phone about the course; I'd already been around it twice, and I was determined to be helpful to everyone who needed us, no matter what our personal circumstances were at the time.

That same weekend, our good friend Charlie Morgan, a contract driver who often works for us, came up and offered to drive our truck and trailer back to Virginia. Knowing that David, the only one in our group who could drive that truck, was in the hospital, he said, "I've got you covered." Better yet, Charlie did it for free, saying, "Don't worry about it. You've got other things to worry about."

David and I believe that people want to be part of something that's bigger than themselves. Perhaps that parallels our Olympic dreams, because at the Games you become a part of something that's bigger than your sport, your team, even your country.

We appreciate those who have a desire to be part of our team, and we're happy to give them credit for it. It pays us back over and over. And we were proud that, in a poll on the grounds of Rolex Kentucky one year, an O'Connor Event Team baseball cap was at the top of the list of things people wanted to acquire during the competition.

We hope the name can continue even when we're not competing—but at that point, it will have to stand for something a little different. Your public personality can't be about the past. It has to be about the future. If you're just trying to live off the past, it never works. We know that the competition thing is fleeting, even if it lasts twenty years—because when it's over, it's not coming back. We'll have to reinvent what we do. There isn't a lot of future in just polishing our trophies and sighing over old scrapbooks.

But it *is* fun to look back and see how far we've come. That includes remembering the bad times as well as the good, because they're all instructive.

So I'll let David fill you in on how badly things were going not too long before the Atlanta Olympics, and the way he persevered to turn them around.

INSIGHT

Building a Competitive Team

Karen and I feel strongly that developing team camaraderie is very important to success in an Olympics, a World Championships, a Pan American Games, or any other event where you are part of a squad.

When you're on a team, though, you've got some hoops to jump through—and you don't have turbo control over it. The team stuff can wear on you; you could very easily get tired of it. To ride for your country is very exciting and thrilling, but it means always having somebody telling you what you can do.

So it's important that you make sure you get what you *(continued)* need out of the team's preparation process. You have to know how *you* are going to get ready. Our attitude is that, whoever you are, once you're named to a team, you have earned the right to be there. If I'm team captain, my job is to make sure you have what you need to give yourself the best chance for a good performance on the day. Everyone is going to need something different; and if it's in our power to give it to you, we're *going* to give it to you. As soon as I'm done with my deal, I'll do whatever you need to help you get ready—and that might be just staying away.

My job is to say "Make sure you are realizing and getting what you need to put your performance at its peak." But I don't tell anybody what they need; they have to tell *me* that.

I try to put people in a comfortable position. For example, I know that a shy rookie may be afraid to put his hand up in the middle of a meeting; after the meeting is adjourned, he might come over to Karen or me and say, "I'm a little confused about how to handle this." When that happens, we go into our consultant mode, saying, "Let's see if we can work this out."

I remember, before the 2002 World Championships in Jerez, Spain, bringing all six of us (the team riders and two individual competitors) together in the barn aisle and talking to everyone. I said, "If we have an amazing day, we're all going to do great. But if we just have a good day, one of us is going to be taken out of the game. We have no idea who, and no idea why. We have to accept that now and deal with it. That's what teamwork is about."

That's an important conversation: Right off the bat, establish the principle of not blaming anybody for a mistake. If you agree to that ahead of time, you're able to deal with the situation. You recognize that the person who has a problem may be you; if it is, you'll want your teammates to be supportive.

To make the team thing work, there has to be a selflessness about each individual. Along with standing up for getting the preparation you believe you need, you have to be selfless in terms of letting irritations roll off like water off a duck's back. There will be days when one person is having a stressful time; everyone else needs to let that happen, especially if you're on a long trip. Everybody gets better at being a people person by the end of one of those trips, because you have to let a lot of stuff go. It's like being in a big family: You learn to overlook a lot.

At the same time, it's important to keep the "team" group as small as possible. Every time you put a new personality into the mix—whether it's a staffer, a parent, or a spouse—you're adding new dimensions. The more there are, the harder it is to cope, and the more you'll find yourself getting distracted. That's why we believe that at the Olympics and World Championships, owners' and parents' access to the competitors should be more limited. In those situations, there's a pressure to get everything done in a short amount of time. If you have outside people begging for your attention, getting everything accomplished winds up being a lot more difficult.

The unique thing about eventing is that it brings a group of individuals together to conduct themselves as a team once a year for three years out of four—at the Olympics, the World Championships, and the Pan Ams. I always go back to what the sport is really all about: You try not to compete against the other competitors. You're competing against the day, handling *that* course under *those* conditions, the dressage test at the time you ride it. If you compete against team members, it becomes very destructive.

The most successful teams have an element of humor throughout the whole trip; people enjoy each other's company. They can rally as a team to keep someone light.

It's rare that everyone on a team is a winner. All we're ever going to ask anyone to do is give it their best shot. If it fails, we're going to be in this together. You won't find us publicly scrutinizing what happened and criticizing the mistakes.

What we both hate, though, is to hear someone who's had a bad performance blaming other factors, either in the process or on the day. That drives us crazy. In the end, you're the one out there on the day, so you're responsible.

CHAPTER THIRTEEN

Sharing a quiet moment with Tex in Sydney

Tex and Tailor

FOUR YEARS AFTER making my international team debut at the first World Equestrian Games, in Stockholm, I found myself at the next WEG in The Hague, Holland, competing as an individual rather than on the team. It wasn't all I had hoped for. On A Mission hurt himself on phase C and didn't jump very well cross-country as a result; we wound up forty-fourth.

At that point, it was obvious I didn't have much left in the way of horses, since Wilton Fair had retired. Jacquie Mars sized up the situation and said, "I think we ought to look around for something for you." And that was how Giltedge and Custom Made came into my life. It's one thing to have one good horse. But to have two with careers like theirs, and to have them play the game the way they did—I was just incredibly lucky.

When we decided to get a new horse, I called William Micklem,

Karen's old instructor. He didn't have many prospects, but he thought it over and then said, "Well, there is Giltex"—a horse who belonged to Irish eventer Eric Smiley.

Karen had actually seen Giltex the year before and thought he was too big for her. We went to look at him and found he was not a great mover, but William said he was a really good galloper and good cross-country horse. I tried him; and though he was not that impressive, Jacquie took a chance and bought him anyway. (She was very good at going on blind faith with us.) It was worth a shot because he wasn't particularly expensive, having been on the market for a long time. We really got him on William's recommendation more than anything else.

When we arrived to see Giltex, we'd been impressed at how beautiful he looked, standing perfectly groomed in the wash stall and already wearing his bridle. It wasn't until we got him home that we learned the hard way that he was impossible to bridle—you couldn't put your hands any further up his face than his eyes. His ears were so sensitive that you couldn't touch them. We spent months taking apart his bridle to put it on him before we were able to get it on without attaching the crownpiece separately. Even then, he only trusted people he knew well to put the bridle on the normal way, without disassembling it.

We never found out why he had the problem with his ears. But once his forelock was braided for a three-day event, we never unbraided it until the end of the weekend, when the competition was over, because rebraiding it daily would have been too traumatic. We didn't want the braider spending more time than necessary in the neighborhood of Tex's ears.

We've often wondered whether Eric presented the horse with a bridle to save time or to save the sale. In that episode, at any rate, Eric taught us that if a horse is bridled when we go to try him, we make sure to take it off and put it on. (Thanks for the tip, Eric.) And actually, he did us a favor in the end. Who knows: If we had learned before we purchased Giltex that it would take twenty minutes to bridle him every time he was

© NANCY JAFFER

My folks, Sally and Jay, were both on hand to support me in Jerez, Spain, for the 2002 World Equestrian Games. All of our parents have played a huge role in our success.

© BRANT GAMMA

Dad cheered us on at Pratoni del Vivaro, Italy, for the 1998 World Equestrian Games. Note the red and yellow lapel ribbons—our team wore them as a gesture of support for Bruce Davidson, who had lost his mother in a car accident right before the Games.

© BRANT GAMMA

The Lendes, Phil and Joanne, have been on Karen's team ever since they gave her her first horse, Midnight, on her eleventh birthday. Now they are an integral part of the O'Connor Event Team in Virginia. Here, they are at the Morven Park Horse Trials with Burghley (left) and Jane Russell.

Karen and I both love teaching youngsters about horses. In this photo from several years ago, I'm introducing Karen's second cousins, Justin and Megan Guarino, to Kingfisher. Justin is now a working student with us in Virginia.

USET director of eventing Jim Wolf and team coach Mark Phillips—up to no good, as usual!

At Burghley for the Open European Championships in 1997, Nash and I were rolling along en route to a clean cross-country round—or so I hoped. Two fences later, though, I suffered a lapse of concentration, and we fell at an easy ditch and brush.

A proud moment for owner, horse and rider: Jacqueline Mars, Tex and I participate in the awards ceremony at Rolex Kentucky in 2001, where Tex was first. His stablemate, Tailor, was third.

Another proud moment, visiting one of Shannon's foals in the pasture at Stonehall Farm. This horse, now called Riverdance, is all grown up and eventing in Colorado with a Young Rider.

Nash, the horse with the greatest heart in the world, and I are on our way to winning the Foxhall Cup in 2001.

David Lenaburg, one of our owners and a great friend, watches while I get a big hug after dressage. It must have gone well!

BIKO

BIKO
USCTA HIGH POINT HORSE OF THE CENTURY
COMPLETED 12 THREE-DAY EVENTS

The ultimate showman, Biko had the last word at his retirement ceremony at Rolex Kentucky in 2001 as he raced around the new Johnson Arena at the Kentucky Horse Park. There were few dry eyes in the house as we galloped around to the music of several songs I had chosen, including Sarah McLachlan's "I Will Remember You." David's brother, Brian O'Connor, also read a poem my dad had written for the occasion.

I have a great interest in and passion for increasing communication with my horses through natural horse-manship. Here, I am working with The Native, a difficult-minded horse who took a lot of time to train. I really enjoyed working with him, though, and probably learned as much from him as he did from me.

In the galloping lane with Grand Slam at Rolex Kentucky 2004.

What a ride: Ponying third-place Tailor, Tex and I take a victory gallop around the arena at Rolex Kentucky in 2001.

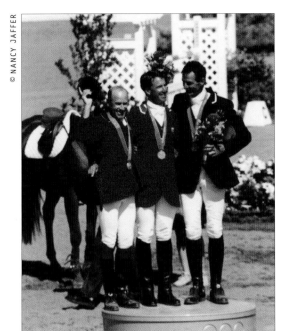

This was a huge moment for me, standing on the podium at Sydney next to the greatest rider of all, Mark Todd, at the end of his career. Silver medalist Andrew Hoy, from Australia, is no slouch, either!

Trailblazers: Tex and I were the first members of the U.S. team to go cross-country in Sydney. We had a clean round, as did Karen and Nash.

The next generation: Taking a quiet moment together before cross-country at Red Hills, Florida, in the spring of 2004 with Outlawed (left) and Upstage.

ridden, we might have missed out on one of the greatest horses Team O'Connor ever had.

Happily, William turned out to be right about Giltex's ability, as he so often was—though it was a while before we knew it. That's the way it goes with horses: If you have time to work and wait, eventually you may find you are riding a whole lot more horse than the one you bought.

Giltex, whom we rechristened Giltedge (we used "Tex" for his stable name), came to America and ran at Fair Hill in the autumn of 1994. Although he was very difficult on the flat, we got a pretty good dressage score. Cross-country, he was very different from the other horses I had ridden; I found myself tapping him with my stick twice in the first three fences to get him to land and go. Coming to the fourth fence, I took my hand off the reins to tap him, and he mistook that as the signal to go. He left the ground and jumped right in the middle of the fence. It was totally my fault, and I paid for it with a lot of shoulder pain after I fell off.

The next year, 1995, I took him to Checkmate in Canada. He was fabulous cross-country until he jumped off an Irish bank. I had figured that, being an Irish horse, he would understand that kind of jump and land more organized than he did. Instead, he took one stride to a short paneled fence, caught the fence with his foot, and flipped. He got off-line or I got off-line; I still don't know what happened. But I wound up with a punctured lung, another painful injury. So in the first two three-day events with him, I'd fallen twice.

I was very discouraged—after all, this was my new toy! I'd thought the horse was getting better and I was learning how to ride him, but things just didn't seem to be going my way. Then we went over to England, where he won some horse trials before I took him to Blenheim. But he pulled a muscle, so I didn't get to run him cross-country.

We brought Tex home for Fair Hill, the one-year anniversary of our first cross-country together (and my fall). Finally, everything clicked; he was second by 0.1 penalties. He just went on to be incredible after that.

In his head, he'd always wanted to do it—he's not a horse who wants to say no. It was just a question of getting his body to catch up to his mind, and to have him understand what I wanted. After Fair Hill, I was never out of the top ten with him again.

Tex became a great favorite of mine in a lot of ways. I like to say that he always shows up for work, and he's done what he's accomplished with less native ability than some other horses have. He's not as naturally talented as somebody like Custom Made, so he has to work harder at it, and he *knows* he has to work harder at it. Mark Phillips called him a "useful" horse. But he won two three-stars and a four-star, and ended up with six medals to his credit. That's pretty good for not being "the most talented." Biko, Eagle Lion, Out And About, and Custom Made were the stars who were supposed to bring home the big medals for the team during the mid- to late 1990s. Well, every time you turned around, Tex was the highest-placed American horse on the team, and he just kept doing it. That's why his victory at Rolex Kentucky in 2001 was such a big emotional win for me and the whole O'Connor Event Team—because it was Tex being the star at last.

Custom Made came to me in sort of the same way as Tex. In 1992, I had returned from England to ride in an event in America, and Joe Zada came up to introduce himself. The horse he had just bought had been taking advantage of him, and he was looking for help. I worked with him at a couple of clinics, and he decided he wanted another horse, so we found Lightfoot, who ended up being fantastic. Joe asked me to do a couple of events with him, and then Lightfoot won Blair Castle and had his own career with me. At that point, Joe said, "Maybe we should have two."

We heard about Custom Made, who was doing Blenheim with a Young Rider, and went to take a look. When I saw him go cross-country there, he ran past two corners; then he had three rails down in show jumping. He was just running off with his rider. But he had a tremendous gallop. People were shying away from buying him because he was fairly strong and not real careful in the show jumping.

I think our deal was clinched when I first looked into the horse's eyes; we had a connection right there. I really liked his appearance; but he was a wide horse, big and round, which made me wonder if he had enough endurance to do the distances. (He's a 7/8 Thoroughbred, but he didn't look it.) I also was worried about how I'd fare with him in the show jumping. But when I jumped him, I found he was a fabulous jumper; he just needed education.

After we bought him, Tailor (as we called him around the barn) and I did some horse trials in the beginning of 1995. He proved to be a very good mover but very aggressive on the cross-country, as I'd witnessed with his former rider at Blenheim. When we went to that year's Rolex three-star, he won the dressage by nearly 12 penalties; then I found myself on a runaway at the end of cross-country. And in show jumping we had a disaster, with 11.5 penalties. Still, we managed to win our first three-day event together, by 0.1 penalties, over Wash Bishop on Ask Away.

After that, I took Tailor to England, where I decided he was really too strong. So I used what's called a Citation bridle, which puts pressure on the horse's nose and keeps the bit high up in the mouth. After I won the Gatcombe Horse Trials with him, I was selected for the US team for the Open European Championships, taking place in the mountains at Pratoni del Vivaro in Italy, which was where the eventing for the World Equestrian Games would be held three years later.

The Citation had been working well in the horse trials, so I used it in the Championships. But there it proved to be our undoing. Tailor had always been spooky at ditches; on the approach to a ditch on cross-country at Pratoni, the ring on the bridle pinched the bit against his mouth and he shot left. I tried to pull him back but, unbalanced, I fell off. That spooked him. He got very aggressive on the rest of cross-country because of his anxiety. (Things used to really bother him.) We got around, but neither of us was very happy.

The unhappiness manifested itself in show jumping the next afternoon. Custom Made hadn't jumped liverpools with me, and in the stadium at Pratoni there were two water trays, one with an oxer built over it. We went to the first water tray slowly, because I was trying to be careful, but he still spooked over it; it probably reminded him of the ditch he had not liked the day before. The next fence was the water tray with the oxer, and at that point there was no way he was going to take it. He'd had enough, and he shut down. We were eliminated.

That had never happened to me before in show jumping, and I was completely devastated. The Olympic Games in Atlanta were only ten months away, and I knew the USET would never trust a horse who was eliminated in show jumping. There was my whole team thing, out the window. It was a horrible trip to Europe.

Wait, there's more.

Worst of all during that season, at the Boekelo event in Holland, I got hit on course by a first-aid worker in a car. He was running late and was supposed to be at his post; there was no crossing guard, and I figured that if this guy looked where he was going, he'd stop. He didn't. He hit me with his front wheel. My horse, Lightfoot, flipped up onto his hood and I broke the windshield with my body.

It was horrifying, but the damage wasn't anywhere near as bad as it could have been. The horse ran off and jumped to safety in a paddock full of cows. I spent the rest of the day alternating between hot baths and putting ice on my back, trying to get it so I could move, because I had to ride Night Rhythm after that. I did go around the course on him—but, to say the least, I wasn't up to form. I had one refusal and was lucky things didn't go any worse.

After that, I needed some time to myself. (When I go through bad periods like these, I generally have forty-eight hours where I don't want to talk to people. Karen handles it in about six hours; we're very different that way.) I felt I needed to find the thread of what I was doing wrong before I made a new plan. I was doubting whether I was good enough to be like one of the people I had looked up to for years and years.

We were supposed to be getting ready for the Olympic Games, but I was wondering whether I was going to make it. In 1992, that horrible year when we lost Mr. Maxwell, I was seventh at Badminton and earned the top points in the selection process with Wilton Fair. (It was a crazy system, but I had taken a chance in going to a four-star, and a decent placing there had earned me more than if I'd won a three-star.) Then, ten days before the Barcelona Olympics, Wilton Fair went lame. I had invested a lot of time and money in trying to make the Olympic squad. Now I was out of the Games and worrying that I'd never get to them, except as a spectator.

When you're trying to make an Olympic Games, whether you wind up going or not, it's in the forefront of your mind for four to eight years. The Olympics aren't just the top of your sport; they're the top of all sporting events, the thing that you're always striving for. When that is taken away from you, for whatever reason, it's a very tough time. You spend a lot of hours reflecting about what you're doing and how you're doing it. Not being able to go to the Olympics can leave a big hole in your life that you have to fill, either with family or new horses or simply getting on with life.

So when things started going wrong in 1995, I started doubting myself, was wondering if I would miss the 1996 Atlanta Olympics, too. Could I ever have a real international sports career? Three weeks in a row, horses that had won horse trials didn't finish three-day events. I was depressed, to say the least.

But things started looking up later in October, when Tex won Fair Hill. And I decided that, step by step, I would start over with Custom Made. So I reintroduced him to all the jumps we'd encounter at an event. Every time I rode him, I made sure he saw a ditch, until he got to the point that he could jump ditches as easily as he could jump a brush fence. We did the same with liverpools.

I knew that my only shot at making the Atlanta Olympics with him was to go to Badminton in May 1996 and do well. I hoped our months of preparation would pay off.

They did.

He won the dressage at Badminton. Then, the next day, we had every kind of weather on phase C of roads and tracks: Microbursts of rain, sun, hail, and snowflakes came through in quick succession. It was a very weird feeling—like "What's up with that?" Nevertheless, Tailor put in a magic cross-country round that was just one second over the time allowed. In show jumping, I had only a single rail down; if I hadn't had that, we would have won. But I was so happy to prove we were back in the game that I didn't mind being third at the toughest annual three-day event in the world.

Tailor and I get along like a house on fire. Maybe that's because he's very much like me: He has a public side and a private side, which he shows by being very grumpy and protective in his stall. He's also a real iron man, and that's what the team selectors call him. He's the toughest horse I've ever met. At the age of seventeen, when he jumped in his last three-day, he was still tough.

In 1996, the US Olympic selectors considered Tailor's record and picked him to compete in the individual eventing medal competition, which would be held for the first time at the Atlanta Games. Prior to that, team and individual medals had been awarded on the basis of the same event, with the best-scoring rider in the team competition getting the individual gold, and so on down the line. But the International Olympic Committee decided that the rule across the board should be "one competition, one medal." That's the way it always worked in show jumping and dressage, where team and individual competitions were separate. Because eventing is so grueling and a horse can do at most two three-days in the course of a year, however, you can't have the same horse/rider combinations in both the team and individual eventing tests at the Games.

The USET decided that they couldn't take a chance on Tailor having problems in the show jumping for the all-important team medal. But they figured that if he was on, I might be able to win the individual prize, and that it was worth taking a chance there.

The O'Connor and Lende families had a lot to look forward to in Atlanta. Karen had made the team with Biko and I'd made the team with Giltedge. So it seemed we'd both finally have the opportunity to show what we could do—after years of frustration as far as the Olympics were concerned.

INSIGHT

Overcoming a Horse's Fear

Think "small" when you're trying to overcome a horse's fear of something, whether it involves riding or stable management or anything else. For instance, if your horse has a ditch problem, you're not going to take him right to a scary ditch. You're going to scale down the exercise until he has more confidence. So you might start with a ditch that's nothing more than a tire rut. From there, you would introduce a ditch that's revetted at one side and sloping on the other side. Make sure he's confident with whatever you have him doing before you move on to the next challenge.

Try to do the easiest thing first to build that confidence. Always start by jumping *up* a bank, rather than down a bank, for instance. If the problem is your horse's reluctance to approach a particular obstacle, start by finding a comfort zone from which he can gradually get closer to a problem obstacle. And start out walking *by* it, not *at* it. Get the two of you used to meeting the stimulus by degrees.

Here's another fear problem that you may encounter: *(continued)*

How many horses are scared by clippers? The noise and vibration they make is huge, and that big power cord can look like a snake. But you can take apart this problem and fix it piece by piece.

First, get an extension cord, gather it in one or both of your hands, and rub it all over him in a gentle manner. When he's OK with that, find something that has a vibration, like those little massage gizmos you can get at Wal-Mart. You could even put a cell phone on "silent," so it vibrates when it rings. Put whatever you're using that vibrates on your horse's shoulder first, then his neck, and finally his muzzle and ears (or whatever other sensitive area you want to clip). When he's got that down pat, start a clipper. Keep it away from him at first, so he can hear the noise and get used to it but not have it on top of him. Then gradually bring it closer, and finally accustom him to the feel as you did with the vibrating gizmo.

Always desensitize in increments. Your efforts will fail if you give your horse too much to absorb too quickly. Rough stuff and using a twitch or tranquilizer are not the answer. Those may be fast fixes that get a job done once, but next time you'll undoubtedly wind up with more trouble than you started with.

Follow this same line of thinking when you're jumping. Start low and narrow to build confidence. Then regulate your challenges by changing height, distance, and width gradually. Make sure you never over-face your horse—or yourself.

Finally, what we find has always helped us the most is not to react to what a horse is doing, but rather to analyze what he is thinking. Put yourself in his head. Think what he thinks; see what he sees. Horses react to their own senses, so become sensitive to how *his* senses operate, rather than relying just on your own reactions. In the end, you're trying to learn the language of your horse, rather than trying to teach him the language of people.

CHAPTER FOURTEEN

Celebrating silver: on the podium with Jill Henneberg and Bruce Davidson

Olympics at Last!

I KNEW I WAS basically always going to be OK in what I did with horses: that I'd be good enough to make a living and be successful to a certain level. But what I *wanted* was to be competitive at the international team level.

As we rang in the New Year of 1996, it was becoming painfully obvious that the centennial Olympics were very much in question for me. Karen is a reactive person who lets go of things and makes the next thing happen. As I've said, I'm more of a planner—and when the plans don't go the way I want, it takes me a while to make a new plan. So I needed a plan as we started to focus on the 1996 Olympics, with the two of us in some ways representing opposite ends of a spectrum.

Up until then, Karen had a more successful career than I did. Biko was coming into his own, and in him she had one of the great horses of the world. She was given a bye from having to go to Rolex Kentucky that spring.

In comparison, in the winter of '95-'96, I wasn't even on the long list, or invited to team training sessions. Tex and Tailor hadn't hit their run yet. Tex had shown his style by winning at Fair Hill, but we had to do more with Tailor. All that just made me work harder. Even going into Atlanta, I still felt as if I needed to take care of Tex a little bit—as if he wasn't quite at the top of the game. But he had still been considered good enough to make the team.

In a way, having a separate individual competition at Atlanta was a bonus for eventing, because we got to have two events—double the exposure—and use different horses for the two competitions. Atlanta was also where my two horses started to get into their roles of Tex being the everyday workman and Tailor being the brilliant one who maybe wasn't so consistent. And this time, having been named to the Olympics with two horses—not just one, who could go lame—I thought that monkey had been knocked off my back.

And it was. Karen and I went to the Games as teammates. It was so wonderful to be able to share the big moments, like getting outfitted for the team. We went in with the volleyballers and the gymnasts, going from one station to another in a big, warehouse-like area. First, they talked to you about conduct—including how to carry the flag, should you get that opportunity. Then they had a dentist check your teeth and a doctor give you a once-over. You got a T-shirt, shoes—all kinds of stuff. The first time you get these team clothes, and they have "USA" written all over them, that's when you really realize that you're finally going to get to play the game you've wanted to play for years—or, in my case, decades. It's really kind of a proud moment, and certainly an exciting moment.

Four days before the Games began, we moved the horses from their training grounds and got our first glimpse of the stadium at Conyers, about an hour from Atlanta, where the equestrian portion of the Olympics would be held. It was such a large stadium that my first impression was "Oh my God, the thing is huge." I figured it would have a real effect on the horses.

The next big impressions involved getting ready for the opening ceremonies after a tour of the Olympic athletes' village. We didn't stay there; we needed to be near the horses, and the village was in downtown Atlanta, so we stayed at a motel in the Conyers area. But we did keep a room in the village for changing our clothes, and we visited the food hall there. It was seven or eight indoor-ring-sized tents, and they were all open, with twenty-four kitchens. You could have whatever kind of food you wanted, from every country. We watched the cyclists eating 8000 calories a day and the gymnasts eating their lettuce leaves. There were Olympians of every size and shape, a veritable smorgasbord of athletes. We felt as if our heads were on swivels as we took it all in. It's just cool being in that environment: All those athletes have gone through the same process in their individual sports that you have in yours. So you have something in common, even if you're an equestrian and they're kayakers.

Getting ready for the opening ceremonies, we sweated in the heat of a baseball-stadium holding area, next door to the main stadium, for about three hours before going in. I was on a ramp about 100 feet from the stadium entrance when the crowd first saw the US women, who went in before the men, led by the American flag. The roar that went up from the packed stadium was amazing. Karen said it gave her the biggest adrenaline rush she ever felt, and I have to agree. It was mind-numbing, an awe-inspiring explosion of sound.

The ramp was on top of the stadium, so we got a great view of 115,000 people, all going absolutely crazy. You forget that you're part of a relatively small sport as you hear the cheers and know that there are millions, maybe billions, more people watching on television.

Once we were in the infield, we were put in corrals. Ours was next to the US basketball "Dream Team." Karen ran into David Robinson and Charles Barkley, two towering players. "Isn't this unbelievable?" she asked them, and they agreed.

Whether you're a pro making a seven-figure salary or someone who struggles every day to pursue a sport that doesn't pay, you develop a special bond with everyone else who has the privilege of being called an Olympian. David and Charles complimented us on our sport—and that stunned us: Everyone was talking about the Dream Team, and yet these athletes had an appreciation for our sport. It made us feel as if everyone was paying attention. I didn't expect that at all.

But Karen's moment with the basketball players was brief. Athletes from a variety of countries, some wearing exotic national dress, were swarming toward the Dream Team, so we made sure we got out of the way.

Two days later, I rode into the dressage arena and Tex put in a good test. Although this was the Olympics, I didn't have any nerves, or even a sensation of where I was, until I made my final salute and left the arena. That was a very emotional time, because the crowd was so supportive and I had done a good enough job. I'm not sure I was looking for the ultimate Olympic performance, because trying too hard can make you screw up. I was just aiming to do the job I knew how to do, and do it well enough to be competitive.

Karen had gone first. Biko, who had never even broken into the 40s in dressage, blew past the 40s and came up with a 38, so we were sharing our pride.

Luckily, being in the huge stadium hadn't had the effect I'd feared when I took my first look at it. I've been in a lot of rings that felt more electric. The deal here was that, because it was so big, when you were out in the middle of the dressage arena, you actually were far away from the crowd. That helped keep the horses calm.

We soon found we were the only American couple who had ever

competed on the same team in the Olympic Summer Games. The distinction got us attention; and once the reporters discovered us, they started to follow us around, which actually turned out to be fun. It was probably the first time that being in the public eye became a responsibility of ours, because we were being interviewed by people outside our sport. That's when we realized we were becoming spokespeople. (We had a little help on the attention front from Bo Derek, best known as the star of the movie *10*, who is really into equestrian sports. A horse owner herself, she told us her biggest moment at the Games was giving Biko a bath.)

While we'd been training in Georgia before heading to Conyers, there had been several injuries among the equestrians, and none of them involved riding accidents. Karen was kicking herself for playing soccer and breaking her left thumb in five places when she should have been focusing on riding in the Olympics. Our teammate Jill Henneberg got dragged by a water-skiing rope and sprained her ankle. There were several more mishaps like that, involving riders from other nations—because what you had was a group of people who were seriously wound up. It was like turning a bunch of fit two-year-old racehorses out together in a field— the last thing you want to do. We found out this sort of stuff is a huge problem for Olympians, so most coaches don't allow people on their teams to do "extracurricular" sports during their training period before the Games. We learned why the hard way.

Karen's thumb turned out to be a big deal. She's left-handed; with her left thumb broken, she needed her right hand to control the horse, which meant she wasn't able to carry a stick cross-country. And Biko, who had never refused, stopped for the first time at the big lake water complex. He jumped into the water fine but missed the step coming out; Karen had no options but to turn and try again. He was a strong horse, and control became more of an issue. Who knew how important the thumb could be in such a situation?

On top of that, the course was a tough ride: The camber, or curvature, of the track, was wrong on a lot of the tight turns. The irrigation also wasn't up to snuff, so that meant there were some deep spots. But, luckily, both Tex and Biko handled it fine.

After we recovered from cross-country, we focused on show jumping, which was going to be a real nail-biter. In the Olympics and WEG, you get to draw from the other equestrian sports to support you. We were helped in our preparation by the US dressage and show-jumping riders. World-famous trainer George Morris and US team coach Frank Chapot, both Olympic medalists themselves, were on hand, too.

Our big problem was that Bruce Davidson's horse, Heyday, wasn't the best show jumper. That meant trouble, because we were looking at winning a silver medal but were only 4 1/2 rails in front of the bronze-medal position—which was being held by the Kiwis, New Zealand's team. It was a ton of pressure, because we knew Heyday would have at least two rails. Jill had been eliminated on cross-country, so we no longer had a drop score. That meant that saving the silver was up to Karen and me.

Biko jumped a great clear round, and Karen and I high-fived each other when she was leaving the ring and I was coming in. The crowd was going crazy at that point. Karen put her finger to her lips and went "Shhhh." Amazingly, that quieted them.

Tex went on to jump a fantastic round. He knew the game by then and showed his competitiveness. (I'd never considered him an exceptional show jumper, but this was the start of a run that had him dropping only one rail in five CCIOs—international team competitions.)

As we had feared, Heyday wasn't jumping that well, but Bruce did a wonderful job with him. Although he toppled four rails, the horse somehow managed to get across the triple combination without error. It was an amazing performance.

We had won the silver by 2 penalties. We just went crazy. This was the first team medal for the US three-day squad at either an Olympics or a World Championship in twelve years. Our dream had come true. And it was even better because, in my case, the person I wanted to share it with was standing right next to me, going through the same emotions.

After we climbed onto the podium, I remember being surprised at how heavy the medal was as it was placed around my neck. Watching the flag go up really puts the fire into you. But it was the Australian national anthem that played for the gold medalists. "The Star-Spangled Banner" was not to be heard that day.

For me, winning a medal was such a relief that I'm not sure I was as competitive as I should have been in the individual competition. In the dressage, for instance, Tailor was second with a good test, but it wasn't his top performance. Still, my experience in Atlanta, playing both games side by side, really helped me do a better job in Sydney four years later. I definitely learned from Atlanta that I needed to switch gears much faster; that's not a normal three-day event. But, as Karen noted, Tailor was going so well in Sydney that it was a motivation in itself. I also was much more organized in my thought process than I'd been in Atlanta.

The Atlanta cross-country course didn't feel like a great one for Tailor, and he lost a shoe. He's a horse that gets stronger as the course goes on; typically we'd be just a little slow at the beginning and try to make it up at the end. I went out in that normal, quiet mode, but I was wrong: On that course I couldn't make it up at the end, even though I was flying. I had just left it too late. We wound up with 30.8 time penalties.

We stood eighth, but we had a shot at a medal going into show jumping. That lasted until we came around to a double next to a TV camera, where Tailor just about stopped when the camera was hoisted up in the air for an overall view of the arena. Trying to scrape through, I had that rail down, then dropped another. That put me fifth: not bad. On the other hand, if I'd left the fences intact, we would have had the individual bronze.

"Oh, well. Next time," I thought—without an inkling that, yes indeed, next time we would take all the marbles.

INSIGHT

Handling a Course

There's a phrase we use to describe any kind of pattern we ride, whether it's a dressage test, a cross-country route, or a show-jumping course. We like to say that they are nothing more than a series of exercises that are connected. Thinking that way helps you break the course down and take it in manageable segments, rather than being overawed by looking at the whole thing.

Remember that every exercise must have a beginning, a middle, and an ending. You cannot start the next exercise until you finish the one you're on. In other words, if you're cantering a show-jumping round, the canter you start your first fence with must be the same rhythm you use to finish the exercise that the first fence is part of. One of the biggest problems in show jumping and cross-country is that horses get away from people because they don't return the horse to a canter that has enough adjustability for them to execute the next exercise.

Let's say the first fence has a connection with the second fence; that's one exercise. You finish that exercise by returning to the canter you started with, even if it's for only a moment, before you start the next exercise, be it a vertical off a corner, a double combination, or something else.

When you walk a course, you'll decide which fences are connected and part of the same exercise. You'll have to decide from the canter you use for one exercise what canter you'll use for the next exercise. And you have all kinds of options; as an example, think about the speed with which you jump up to answer the phone, as opposed to the speed with which you carry a tray of crystal into a room.

Test yourself and your horse as thoroughly as possible before you enter a competition. If you can't go from canter to halt in one stride in dressage, in one or two strides in show jumping, in three to five in cross-country, and in five to ten in steeplechase, then you don't have a horse that's on his feet. A horse should never be out of control of his own body, and there's no point in competing until he's *in* control.

You also have to be able to know how to put your horse into a gait that's adjustable to a number of different tasks. Each task has its own specifics of direction, speed, balance, and rhythm. When we walk a course, we look at the different exercises in that context.

We will have asked all the basic questions of the horse in training before we go to a competition. These questions might mutate into a different-looking form on course, but they're the same questions we've dealt with in schooling, whether it's a one-stride set at 24 feet or 21 feet, a vertical to oxer or oxer to vertical, taking a fence uphill or downhill, or whatever.

It's important to introduce all those exercises to your horse in a training atmosphere before he has to tackle them in a competitive atmosphere. That way, neither you nor he will be intimidated by the fact that, when you get to a competition, the vertical is a flag of wavy-looking planks, or the oxer is flanked by standards that look like the clubhouse spires at Churchill Downs. However a fence is framed, remember that it's the same question; it's just been given a different look. And take heart from the fact that in show jumping, there are only so many different things you can be asked to do.

If you're the person who's preparing a horse to compete, it's key that you give him enough information beforehand so the competition doesn't overwhelm him and/or his rider. In today's industry, there are so many schooling shows and cross-country days and other ways to introduce these exercises in a schooling atmosphere. Take advantage of them—and, for example, never ask a horse to do his first ditch or water in a competition atmosphere. Doing so, you'd be setting the two of you up for failure, because you wouldn't have the tools to negotiate the exercise. You want to keep things simple and fun for him, not have him overwhelmed by an exercise because you haven't introduced it properly. That's a recipe for disaster.

CHAPTER FIFTEEN

©BRANT GAMMA

Nash in dressage, which improved as our partnership evolved

Prince Panache

WHILE DAVID WAS WORKING with his pair of talented stablemates, Tex and Tailor, I was busy with another special duo: Biko and Prince Panache.

In 1992, I had asked Susie Pragnall, a very sharp British horsewoman, to give me a shout if she came across a nice two-star horse. And that was how we found Prince Panache. To a point, I took him on faith because of Susie's recommendation. We got to see him only in the small outdoor arena, and he was very unimpressive on the flat. His canter needed a lot of work: Not only was it four-beat, but when he circled on the right-lead canter, he switched behind all the time; I was concerned about how long getting him to come around would take. But when he jumped, he was very scopey. I did like that.

Susie advised, "You're going to have to trust me on the cross-country. He's one of the nicest cross-country horses I've ever seen." I called Jacquie and said, "This is one I really like."

When it came time for Nash's vetting, he was lame. He'd sustained a nasty cut on the coronary band after grabbing himself. We had to judge whether the lameness was a temporary thing or a long-term problem. We decided to take the chance.

I first competed Nash in the summer of 1993 and planned to take him to a three-star in the autumn. At the time, I was also riding a mare named Shannon, another of Jacquie's horses, who'd been successfully campaigned by Michael Godfrey when Jacquie lived in New Jersey for a while. Shannon and I had won Ireland's Punchestown three-star in the spring. We decided to compete both her and Nash at Fair Hill, because Boekelo in Holland had gotten canceled and there were no other fall three-day events at that time.

At Fair Hill, Shannon won the dressage but slipped and ran out on cross-country. Nash, however, did well enough for me to finish the year third in the FEI International Rider rankings, and first among the women riders, which was a big deal for me. And David won Fair Hill, with Wilton Fair, in what really was "Wilbur weather": an intense downpour on cross-country day that fazed the big horse not at all.

That was Wilbur's final competition. At the end of cross-country, after he'd been so great, I couldn't tell whether that was rain or tears streaming down David's face.

Shannon, now sixteen, was also retired after Fair Hill. She went off to be a broodmare in Ireland, along with Winter's Tale, another mare Michael had ridden for Jacquie. (Their babies are among the horses we've been bringing along in recent years.)

The next spring, looking ahead to the World Equestrian Games in Holland, we were based at Gatcombe, my old stomping grounds in England. Competing at Althorp, the family home of Princess Diana, I was riding Nash first and Biko second. Mark Phillips suggested taking more of an angle at a corner fence than I'd ever practiced or been comfortable with. Because I respected his opinion so much, I followed his suggestion with Nash, who ran out. So with Biko I went with my gut, took the line *I* was comfortable with, and it worked out. That was an important lesson to learn: how to blend your gut feelings with the expertise of the people around you.

So Nash didn't make the team for the World Equestrian Games but Biko did; he finished eleventh there. Nash, however, got to go to Burghley, the autumn four-star, where he came in fifth—even though he still wasn't very good in the dressage.

Nash has always been loving and sensitive: a lovely horse to be around, who would try his heart out for you. Although he was athletic, he was not that easy on himself physically, so mastering the management of his soundness took a long time.

By 1998, Nash was an established equine celebrity. We found ourselves on the team, along with David and Tex, at that year's World Equestrian Games—in Pratoni del Vivaro, Italy, scene of the problematic 1995 Open European Championships. This time, with three more years of training under our belts and Olympic medals to our credit, we were ready for big things.

At Pratoni, I had both Biko and Nash ready. However, the selectors felt that on the narrow twisting and turning course, the more compact Nash would be able to handle the terrain better than the bigger, long-strided Biko. Karen Stives, the 1984 Olympic individual silver medalist who headed the selectors, questioned me as to which horse I should be running that weekend. I replied, "Well, if you're asking which one I could go faster on, I could go faster on Nash. The course is quite hilly and turny, and I think I could turn in a more competitive round on Nash."

When word of that conversation got back to the Thompsons, who owned Biko, they were upset that I wasn't riding their horse. That was disappointing to me. I'm not a selector, so I didn't have the final say. And my being asked which horse I'd prefer to ride at Pratoni was like a parent's being asked to pick between two of her children. I'd have been honored to ride either horse.

Custom Made was still recovering from a 1997 tendon injury, so Tex fulfilled his now-customary role for David as a team horse at the WEG. He was great all the way around. He did a good dressage test. Cross-country, he really fought for it over the longest course he'd ever run, never putting a foot wrong. (He wound up being tied for fifth with a fantastic clear show-jumping round: the best-scoring American horse, again.)

Everyone on the team had rallied around Bruce Davidson, our lead-off rider, because his mother had died in a car accident just before the Games. He had to fly home for the funeral, then fly back to Italy to compete. We all wore lapel ribbons in yellow and red, Bruce's stable colors, to show our support. So there was a lot going on as I went out on phase A in the pouring rain.

Nash was feeling great as we moved onto the steeplechase course—but by the second or third fence, he was slowing down. That was very unusual, because he generally went like a freight train. By the time I got to the fifth or sixth fence, he'd just about broken to the trot.

It was a scary situation. I was on the team, and my job was to finish, but I couldn't even keep him going. I jumped the last fence, and then he did break to a trot before the finish line.

Suddenly, I wasn't thinking about the competition any more. I was scared for my horse's life. I didn't want to pull him up quickly, since I really didn't know what was happening. I kept him trotting, not wanting him to collapse. Finally I dismounted and led him to the assistance area, where US vet Cathy Kohn whipped out her stethoscope.

I told her, "I think there's something wrong with his heart."

She listened to the beat for a minute and said, "He's in A-fib."

"What is that?" I asked, perplexed and scared.

"His heart's in atrial fibrillation. Don't panic, though. It's not a dying situation."

We got Nash into a trailer and back to the stables, leaving the team with no fourth rider and no drop score. David, who had been watching the steeplechase, was right there to put a hand on Nash's heart and comfort me.

We were disappointed, because we'd thought we were going to have a good performance, but we'd been around long enough to know that luck goes up and down. Those disappointments are a huge part of the team thing: On a good day, you lose one person. On an average day, you might lose two. On a bad day, you get three people taken out. On an exceptional day—which maybe happens once in your career—you get all four of you jumping around clear.

At the stables, the vets gave Nash fluids and electrolytes and his heart reverted to its normal rhythm. We never found out what caused the problem. He had a heart murmur, which I knew about, so I would have thought the two were related; but the heart specialist said there was no conclusive evidence to prove that.

With only three riders left on our team, we wound up in fourth place—but not for long. One of the British horses came up positive for a forbidden substance, so they eventually lost the bronze medal and we got it. The consequences of a positive drug test are huge. I have no problem with backing into a medal, because the rules are the rules.

Something negative usually has a positive effect, too. In this case, the incident, although highly controversial, had a beneficial significance for the sport in the long run. It demonstrated that eventing is on the up-and-up, that cheaters are punished, and that we do govern our own sport to the highest standards for the safety of our horses.

In the short run, unfortunately, the controversy surrounding this particular incident dragged on, and dragged the sport into a mess.

Another sad aspect of it for us was that Nigel Taylor—who had nothing to do with the drugging—was on the British team, and this had been his first medal. We're close to Nigel because he's married to our old friend Ann Hardaway, so we wound up taking a medal off someone we didn't want to see lose it.

And I won a medal without having my score count. A lot of people have made their careers on that, though, and in one way, it's a cool feeling: having your teammates hold up your end for you. It was a way to have something positive happen out of what was such a negative weekend for me personally.

We had to really concentrate on Nash's welfare at this point. I thought, "We've already had to manage Nash limb to limb; now, in addition, he's had a problem with his ticker." We took him to the University of Pennsylvania's New Bolton Center, and the cardiologist there, Dr. Jenny Reef, took a real interest in him. He went up to New Bolton every four or five months, and the people from there really enjoyed following him.

After Nash started having soundness problems, Biko's soaring career overshadowed him. We had to wait for diagnostic and treatment technology to catch up to Nash's needs. When it finally did, he had a stellar record.

Nuclear scintigraphy helped pinpoint Nash's problems: He had a hind-end hitch, he'd fractured the wingtip of his coffin bone, and he always had muscular issues. But by the final Olympic trial in 1996, I'd given up on him for the time being; I was just behind the curve on managing him.

Not until 1997 did this state of affairs start to change, something that coincided with Dr. Kent Allen's moving into town and becoming our veterinarian. From 1997 until spring 2001, Kent and his team had a dramatic effect on the veterinary management of Nash's career. We got better at handling his problems, figuring out everything from the details of his shoeing to a maintenance program that worked for him. We didn't leave out any method that might help a horse, including homeopathic remedies, acupuncture, and electromagnetic therapy—all those different techniques that can help stimulate healing and promote circulation.

So one of the biggest ups of my career came when, in 1999, I won the Rolex Kentucky four-star on Prince Panache. He had really come back, thanks to the help of so many people and to his own determination. As I said at the time, not only was his heart not a problem; he actually had the biggest and greatest heart in the world.

Are We Having Fun Yet?

When people say to you, before you go cross-country, "Have fun," what you want to tell them is "If I were going to have fun, I'd be going on vacation to the Caribbean, or scuba diving, or playing golf."

Being on a team is as if you've been hired to do a job. It isn't *about* fun.

Not that there aren't some fun aspects to cross-country; for example, it *is* really neat to drop down over a big fence into water. But it also is really hard. Basically, it's just what we're trained to do as competitors: to run around 4 1/2 miles of cross-country, over awe-inspiring jumps, do it inside the time—and, if we can, act cool about it.

All of us who do three-day events walk to phase A on our horses with butterflies in our stomachs. We look at each other, the old guys especially, and say, "Why do we do this?" If we see someone who's retired from competition and is now there just to coach or watch, we might ask him, "You really miss this feeling, don't you?" and get a knowing laugh in return.

But the other aspect of the situation is how it feels after you've successfully completed cross-country—when your adrenaline is still up and you know you've achieved something. For us, it's the greatest sporting challenge we've ever had the privilege to participate in.

You might wonder at this point: Do we love what we do? There's no question—the answer is yes.

CHAPTER SIXTEEN

With Tailor on cross-country at Burghley

A Winning Streak

COMING OFF OUR Olympic medal in 1996, Karen and I faced a question: what to do in 1997 for an encore. The year after the Olympics is always the slowest of the quadrennium, the only year without a major international championship. But I had a goal. Having finished third at Badminton in 1996, I wanted to win it, and Tailor was ready.

I started out tied for second in dressage at this famous four-star, behind England's Ian Stark and Stanwick Ghost. And, as I had in 1996, I scored just 0.4 time penalties cross-country. That put me second on my own, still behind Ian.

"At least I'm moving in the right direction," I told Mark Phillips. In jumping, Tailor was perfect over the fences, getting only 0.25 time penalties. Meanwhile, Ian had a mere two faults in hand, and he was riding a notoriously bad show jumper. When I came out of the ring, I looked up at Ian and he was looking back at me and shaking his head. I knew he didn't have it.

I remember telling him as our paths crossed, "You've got to give your all," but he and I knew right then that I had won it, even though he had not even started off through the timers yet. And sure enough, he had five rails down.

Still, I was shocked as it finally sank in that I had won Badminton. "Who would have thought I would be standing here?" I was saying to myself as I rode into the center of the arena for the awards presentation.

The feeling was as great as I thought it would be. It's one of those instances where you suddenly become part of a very small, exclusive club. New Zealander Blyth Tait, the Olympic champion, came up to me afterward and said something really nice: "A lot of times, people win these things and they're not true four-star riders, but I want you to know right now that you are."

Win or lose, I've always enjoyed Badminton. It's like playing the Masters in golf, or going to Wimbledon in tennis—it's the top of the game. I don't think the course is necessarily the toughest in the world every year, but it's the one with the most history. That makes it very special to me.

Accepting that trophy was quite a moment, I can tell you. I had won a lot of three-stars, but this was my first four-star. When you've been on top in one of the big ones, no one can ever take that away from you. I finally felt I was *competing* at the four-star level, not just getting up there and hitting or missing.

But things change fast in this game. At the Open European Championships at Burghley that fall, Tailor tripped in the first water jump, had two stops on cross-country, and dropped five rails in show jumping (shades of Stanwick Ghost!).

I was riding with a broken collarbone that I'd sustained with

Lightfoot a week earlier at Blenheim, so my control wasn't what it should have been. But the reason why Tailor had stopped didn't become obvious to us until he came out of quarantine in the US after two days without our care (quarantine stations do not allow non-government employees to enter). That's when we found he'd strained a tendon at the Championships. The injury put him out of action for at least six months. Luckily, I had Tex to fill in the gaps.

Tex and I had another of our great experiences at the 1999 Pan American Games. (OK, they're not as big a deal as the Olympics, the WEG, or even Badminton, but they're still pretty cool.) I took them really seriously, because the US hadn't won a Pan Am gold in quite a long time. The Brazilians had beaten us in the last Pan Ams, in Argentina in 1995. That was a trip I didn't get to make, even though I'd been selected for the team with Lightfoot. I was packing to get ready when I got a call from Mark Phillips after the horses arrived in Miami, on their way to South America. "I've got some really bad news," he said. "Lightfoot's lame, and we think he's done a tendon."

What a letdown. I had been really excited, because I had never done a Pan Am Games or gone to Argentina. So I stayed home.

Now, four years later, I had another chance at a Pan Am medal (in Winnipeg this time), and I thought we needed a medal, morale-wise, in the lead-up to the Olympic Games. (That's what the Pan American Games are for: a huge morale booster.)

In Winnipeg, we had a great run. We got the team gold, and I won the individual silver. I missed the gold because I had a rail down in show jumping with Tex; it went to Mary Jane Tumbridge of Bermuda, on the aptly named Bermuda's Gold. The US's Abigail Lufkin got the individual bronze.

Sadly, Bermuda's Gold would die a year later at the Olympics. At the third fence on the individual event's cross-country course, the bay mare snapped her left front foreleg; you could see the awful wobble instantly when she landed. The diagnosis was multiple fractures of the upper cannon bone and damage to the knee. The fourteen-year-old Thoroughbred was taken to a veterinary clinic and put down after the fracture was found to be inoperable.

That was the only real rain on our parade at the Olympics in Sydney, where I won my individual gold with Tailor after the team earned bronze with Karen riding Prince Panache and me aboard the very veteran Tex.

The road to those medals was a tough one, because we were in Australia for months. Our life during those months wasn't hard, though: We stayed at a wonderful facility owned by multimillionaire Kerry Packer, one of those larger-than-life people you'll never forget.

Kerry's property was 80,000 acres on the edge of the Outback, 40 miles from the nearest town. What he'd done to ensure a high standard of living for his employees was, essentially, to build a town on his land. It had its own restaurant, gym, theater, and go-kart track; and while we were there, a Greg Norman golf course was under construction. There were eight or nine beautiful polo fields, one of which was high enough that even though we had a wet spring, the footing stayed quite good. So we had plenty of amenities—and anyway, we were so busy with the horses that being six hours from Sydney didn't matter.

Unfortunately, off the polo field, the terrain was quite rugged. So the time in training took its toll, and we lost several of our horses to injury. Tailor was almost one of them when he got kicked in the hock by his stablemate, Rattle 'N' Hum, while out for a hack. The injury looked very serious, because it had opened his joint capsule. Not only did he seem unlikely to start in the Olympics, but his future was also a real concern. But veterinarian Mark Revenaugh, who attended him, saved the day, repeatedly flushing the joint with a sterile saline solution and antibiotics. He kept a close watch over his patient until the moment Tailor could finally take his first gallop and resume training.

When Tailor earned the gold medal, Mark unfortunately wasn't on hand, but he got the first phone call with the news—and a case of champagne for his efforts.

After our team earned the bronze medal, Karen and I were together on an Olympic podium for the second time. I grabbed her hand while we stood there, listening to the cheers of the crowd, and told her to hang onto the moment, explaining, "I don't know if we'll ever be up here again."

It was quite extraordinary that we had shared two such times, in Atlanta and Australia. Being married to your teammate intensifies the glory, making the most of an already incredibly special experience.

INSIGHT

Getting Ready for a Successful Jumping Test

When you're preparing to tackle a show-jumping course, you generally can accomplish the job with the help of just four categories of exercises.

The first category is a series of adjustability exercises, involving lengthening and shortening stride. (We practice these all the time, both on the flat and over fences.) The second category is exercises that teach your horse to jump and turn. The third group teaches him to jump questions requiring more accuracy, such as corners and narrow fences. (Though there are no corners in show jumping, you need to introduce this test in the ring, in a show-jumping atmosphere. You can't expect success if you just go out on a cross-country course and jump a corner!) The last group of exercises, more targeted for cross-country but used from time to time in show jumping, are those that get him comfortable with jumping on an angle.

Within those groups of exercises, you can mix and *(continued)* match what you do to increase the level of difficulty in a schooling atmosphere and over a variety of different jumps. Before you walk your first related distance, you will need to understand your horse's length of stride and how it relates to the distances you will encounter on that day. If you walk a distance of 55 feet between two jumps, for example, you need to know that's 5 feet short of a normal four-stride; if your horse has a normal stride, you'll have to go slow to it. That's giving him and you the best chance of understanding the exercise. You just don't run on down to the first fence and see what happens—those days are long gone.

Another requirement for being good at show jumping and show-jumping courses is being able to understand how the variables will affect your trip that day. "Variables" include the type of jumps, how brightly painted they are, the terrain, the footing, the size of your horse relative to the jumping area, and how brave he is (or not) on that day. So test your tools of adjustability—in other words, lengthen and shorten him, before you even start your course.

Any time you're unsure of your horse's confidence, the best thing you can do is go into the arena and make the most of the time you have before you go through the start flags. Tour the arena to let him get a look at what's in there and the crowd around it (if there is one) while you repeatedly lengthen and shorten him at the canter, making him more adjustable and responsive to your requests.

As you go up the levels of competition with your horse, you need to be increasingly responsible for and in control of the line of direction. At the lowest level, you want to get around your corners without having him shy or go sideways. At the highest level, you should be within an inch of where you want to be at takeoff.

CHAPTER SEVENTEEN

© NANCY JAFFER

Kim, Amy, John, and I show off our gold

Finally, Team Gold

AFTER THE SYDNEY OLYMPICS, the next big championship—the 2002 World Equestrian Games in Jerez, Spain—looked like a huge question mark for the US Equestrian Team. The British were as strong as they'd ever been, the French were great, and the Australians were expected to walk away with it. Meanwhile, the three people with me on our squad were new to the international-championship team experience: Kim Severson (who was Kim Vinoski at the time), John Williams, and Amy Tryon. As a group, we were short on proven stars, and I think some of the other countries didn't take us seriously because of that.

The cross-country course, built at an army base a short drive up the mountains from the city, was one of the hardest we've ever jumped. For Giltedge, it proved to be the pinnacle of his career.

We made a mistake before he started cross-country by not putting big enough studs in his shoes to give him a grip on turf that turned out to be slicker than we expected. I went early as the US team's pathfinder, so we weren't really sure what we needed; when I got out there, he started slipping behind. Tex is a horse that needs to get into a rhythm, and the slipping made him tired because he had to fight so hard to jump and get out of those turns on that twisting course. A lot of horses would have given up mentally in that situation, but what Tex did was above and beyond the call of duty. To me, it showed him at his finest.

When Tex slipped the second or third time, I knew we weren't going to be able to come within 10 seconds of the time. I realized it wasn't a day when I was going to beat the course, even though I knew I could have under the right circumstances. But when you're riding for a team, you're there to do a job, not go for individual glory. My responsibility was to get across the finish line: to produce a round that would get me home with the least faults possible. So I readjusted the game plan and turned into a fighter.

As we went along the undulating terrain, I thought the course was very punishing, confirming the assessment I'd made after we walked it the day before. At that time, I felt I didn't want to jump the big water the straight way because I didn't think it would work. But when I came into the 10-minute box, just before I took off on cross-country, Mark Phillips told me that it was jumping fine. And I knew that if any horse could jump it, Giltedge could.

The test involved coming down a steep hill and jumping onto and off of an island in the water. The biggest crowd on the course was surrounding the jump, because it was nearly as scary (and exciting) to watch as it was to ride.

Taking a deep breath, Tex and I slid down that hill and into the water. We jumped the whole thing perfectly. Then, just as I was congratulating myself, I missed my rein coming out and nearly ran straight into the crowd before I got back on my line.

When I finally dismounted after making it safely over all the jumps, I took stock of what we had just done. OK, so we had 30.40 time penalties—I was just glad we'd made it through this test. The route was so twisty and turny and out of rhythm that it was punishing. To me, the horses seemed more tired and mentally exhausted here than they'd been at Sydney, and Sydney was a minute and a half longer. But Sydney was a galloping course, forward into a rhythm, so they could really come home feeling that they'd achieved something.

When I watched the tape of the day at Jerez, I was horrified at the problems so many of the teams encountered. We had predicted it would be a bad day, but we hadn't predicted a bad day for ourselves because we had good jumpers and good riders. Of course, that doesn't mean it was a good day for the sport. I was just glad we beat the course.

Kim on Winsome Adante and John on Carrick had both done a beautiful job. In fact, John was in the lead after cross-country. Amy's horse, Poggio II, gets unridable sometimes, and he did it at the wrong moment at the WEG. But although Amy took a bad fall at the Euro complex of obstacles, fracturing a vertebra in her back, she bravely climbed back on and finished. *That's* being a team player.

"In my ten years since I came here [to the USET]," said Mark Phillips, "this is the best squad, the best team, of horses and riders that I've had. There's a really good spirit and atmosphere among the riders."

I agreed: This was the best team I've ever been around, and I've been around a couple. This was a real team effort in every aspect, from support to morale to riding, and behind the scenes as well. It was an honor for me to ride with these guys.

The next day, Tex put in a clean show-jumping round—one of only five—and I felt a twinge of nostalgia, because I knew this was going to be his last international three-day. He had delivered, as he always did. You could not ask more of a horse than he had given for me all these years.

Among the other riders, though, rails had been dropping like pickup sticks. Amy, riding in tremendous pain, had one down; Kim had three down. But our lead after cross-country was so huge that we were pretty comfortable. John, riding last, had two rails in hand to clinch the individual gold medal, but he dropped the first two fences. Then he had two more down, putting himself out of the medals. But what mattered was that we had the team gold.

We came and beat the world, and we beat them fair and square. We'd been building toward that gold medal for a long time. It was a culmination—and nice to be able to say that, for once, we came away with the big prize.

From a historical point of view, 1974 was the first international championship I ever saw, watching Bruce Davidson win the World Championships at Burghley as the US team took gold. Actually getting to win one myself, twenty-eight years later, closed another circle, like my circle made by my having been at the beginning and end of Mark Todd's career. I like those circles; they give me comfort because they put everything in perspective. You realize that you're no better or worse than other people who have done it before, or than other people who will do it again.

I thought the WEG gold was quite an achievement, so I figured we'd come back to a welcome like the one we had after the Olympics, where we were overwhelmed at the reception we received. When we got off the plane in Washington from Sydney, a hundred of our closest friends were there, and I was truly bowled over.

But the WEG didn't turn out to be as big a deal as I expected. The media hadn't covered it, and it seemed as if the public didn't really care. Most people are expecting us to medal now, I guess. Then, too, the WEG was held during the height of the US football season, so the media and the public were preoccupied with other things.

The 2002 WEG was a demarcation line, the end of eight years of effort by a wonderful group that worked together, going for the gold. They included veterinarians Brendan Furlong and Cathy Kohn, therapist Doug Hannum, Mark Phillips, USET Eventing Activities Director Jim Wolf, and so many others—including the very hard-working selectors. Karen was part of the group, too. At the WEG, her involvement was amazing; I thought she handled herself with incredible grace through the whole trip. She ended up being as much of a team member as anyone else, even though she wasn't riding.

Karen hit just the right note with the extent of her participation. As she said, she was very conscious of the fact she was not a team member. That's a private club, and it's supposed to be. But because we had a young team in terms of international mileage, she could offer its members her experience in logistical planning to make their lives easier. Mark embraced her intellect and opinion on the jumps when they walked the course.

Karen hadn't made this team because Regal Scot, who'd been short-listed for the WEG with her, had a shoulder problem. He was a hard-luck horse if there ever was one—but I'll let her tell that story.

Giving Back to the Sport

Both Karen and I were brought up with the credo that you should give back to your sport. We each have done committee work for years, for the American Horse Shows Association and its successors, USA Equestrian and the US Equestrian Federation, and for the US Eventing Association.

I was a US Equestrian Team product, so that organization was always important to me also. But when USA Equestrian and the USET started to fight over which should be the national governing body (NGB) of horse sports, I didn't feel that the model the USET was presenting was going to work. I thought having the USET be the NGB would fragment the sport.

After having won a couple of medals in a row, I was in the difficult position of speaking against the organization that had done so much for me. My doing so certainly took some people by surprise, but I was adamant in my belief. So I stepped up and, as part of a compromise solution, offered to lead the new United States Equestrian Federation—and it worked.

There's no question that I became the leader of the Federation because I'm the middle guy, the compromise guy. I'm the one both sides ended up talking to. It was a role that made sense because I was an active athlete. One of the things that had helped as I tried to bring the USET and USA Equestrian together is the fact that I'm not an instant-reaction person. When someone blows up at me, I tend to go "uh-huh" and let him keep talking. If you allow people to ramble on, they'll end up talking themselves into the answer. I tend not to react with people when they're going through their emotional stage. I might have to just be patient for weeks or months before getting results, but I can. It's something I learned from dealing with horses.

Any time you get put in a leadership position and you can solve problems, that makes you feel good about yourself and makes you believe you can do things. However, I don't see my job as president of the Federation as all that different from the way we run our team here at home. My job is not to run the Federation. There are lots of good people who do that: technical people to handle the details. I'm a cheerleader, not a micro-manager. What I have to do is put a face and a smile and a captaincy on the Federation.

CHAPTER EIGHTEEN

Competing with Scotty at Fair Hill

Hard Times

A S I LOOK BACK on my career, the highlights are obvious—my marriage to David, the two Olympic medals we shared, victory at Rolex Kentucky, and all the other big wins that meant so much.

But to put it in perspective, I also remember the hard times. They include my severe injuries at Burghley in 1987, the disaster of the 1988 Olympics, and the death of Mr. Maxwell. Just as difficult in its own way was my experience with Regal Scot, a very special horse whose myriad physical problems kept him from reaching his potential.

In the spring of 1999, Jacquie called me for a conference, concerned that Nash might not be able to do everything we wanted to do because of his heart condition. Both he and Biko were fifteen at that point. With my international-level mounts getting older, she thought we should consider whether there was a horse already doing well in events that she could purchase for top-level ventures. And then she wondered whether the Thompsons would like to be part of the deal. This was just another example of how the O'Connor Team spirit continued to grow.

At the time, I had just gotten my issue of *Eventing* magazine, which is published in Great Britain, and read about a horse named Regal Scot. He had won Boekelo and then Punchestown with Mark Todd. A photo of Scotty in the article showed him looking great over a jump. I called Mark's cell phone and got him as he was walking the cross-country course at Bramham.

"Would you consider selling Regal Scot?" I asked, thinking he might possibly say yes because he and his wife, Carolyn, were planning to move back to New Zealand within the year for Mark to pursue his new career as a racehorse trainer.

His answer surprised me.

"The horse is not mine to sell," he told me. "It's actually Carolyn's horse, and I can't imagine she'll sell him."

Regal Scot had been shipped over to Britain by boat from New Zealand as a young horse. He'd needed a year to recover from that very trying three-week journey over the ocean. (That, it turned out, was a harbinger for the rest of his life: He spent as much time sick or injured as he did healthy.)

When Regal Scot arrived in England, Carolyn took him out of Mark's program and made him her project. He didn't go back to Mark until she had competed in an Advanced horse trials with him—and spent hours and hours rehabilitating, nurturing, and riding him.

Carolyn and I talked back and forth about Regal Scot for about a month. Finally, she agreed to sell him to us. She knew he was a valuable horse and figured I was the one who should have him if she was going to sell him. The money from his sale went to her mother as a retirement annuity, but she did ask if we would send him back to her when we were through competing him, and I agreed.

I liked Regal Scot from the minute I first rode him, and I was so glad that Jacquie and the Thompsons were able to buy him. In the fall of 1999, he tied for first place at Fair Hill with David's horse Rattle 'N' Hum. But he wound up with the second-place ribbon when the tie was broken in Rattle 'N' Hum's favor because David was closer to the optimum time on cross-country.

It was a relief to have done so well with Regal Scot in our first three-star together. I couldn't wait to have that behind me, because there was so much pressure with everyone watching to see how my partnership with Scotty would compare to Mark Todd's performance with him. On top of that, I no longer had Biko in my string. At Burghley that year, disaster had struck when he was two-thirds of the way around the course: On a turn after a jump, it suddenly felt as if his whole hind end had gone out from under him. He had slipped the Achilles tendons off both his hocks. And that ended the career of the US Eventing Association's Horse of the Century. (Today he enjoys himself in a pasture with his old pal Nash. Both have earned their relaxation, and they're happy in their field with plenty of grass and a great view of one of the most beautiful areas of Virginia.)

I thought I was off to a fine start with Scotty, and he went well all through the spring of 2000. He ran by an element of a combination at Rolex Kentucky, but the selectors put him on the short list for the Sydney Olympics anyway. That summer, while we were in our US quarantine for Sydney, the idea was always that if he got the chance, he'd run on the team and Nash would run for me in the individual competition. That was my goal, anyway.

But Scotty never got on the plane for Sydney. He turned out to have a cyst in his left hind fetlock. This wasn't the ganglia type of cyst you might be familiar with. Instead, it was literally a decaying hole in the bone. Heartbroken, we thought it was the end for Scotty. It was the most painful thing, both for him and for those who were taking care of him at home while I was in Australia, riding Nash with the team.

Scotty was in so much pain that he went catatonic. I got a call from Sue Clark on the morning of my dressage test in Sydney, saying that they didn't know if they could get him through the day and asking my permission to do what they had to do. A vet, meanwhile, was trying to put together a chemical narcotic to see him through, but there was a fear that a drug of that magnitude could shut down Scotty's organs.

Though given with much trepidation, the narcotic did turn him around. At least, we thought, he could have a peaceful life as a pasture ornament. We collected on the loss-of-use insurance for him, which paid only half his value, and resigned ourselves to the idea that he would never compete again.

Then, in 2001, shock-wave therapy came on the scene: the latest, greatest technology for bringing circulation to a very focal point by means of high-pressure acoustic waves that make the body react to that focal area. The technique was being used successfully to break up kidney stones. We tried it on Scotty, and it broke up the cyst!

We kept taking X-rays to track the progress of Scotty's healing. We saw the hole filling in; six months later, we couldn't see it all. After more than a year off, Scotty was back in action.

In 2002, he got legged up and was having a great spring. We had high hopes for that year's Rolex Kentucky, but I was the first one out on cross-country on a very rainy day, and we were off our line from what everyone thought the water jump would ride like. I saw it too long, he hung a leg, and I fell off. My foot was caught in the stirrup, a very dangerous position to be in, but stalwart Scotty stood stock-still until I could be extricated.

The selectors forgave me for that mishap, and after a good run at Bramham in England, we were short-listed for September's World Equestrian Games.

Then one day, Scotty came out of his stall crippled in his shoulder.

An X-ray located another cyst. It was the same kind as the one in his fet-lock, though not nearly as bad. I couldn't believe it. "This horse is just plagued with bad luck," I thought sadly. But shock-wave therapy once again worked its magic, although (as David's told you) not soon enough for Scotty to make the trip to Spain for the WEG. So we set our sights on Badminton for the spring of 2003.

Sadly, the cloud over his head continued to shadow him. Once we were at Badminton, I was thinking I'd finally get a chance to show what Scotty and I could do together. I decided to hack up to the arena with Blyth Tait, an old friend. Unfortunately, Blyth's horse spooked and banged straight into Scotty's hip, injuring him. That meant he couldn't run at Badminton. So we decided to follow the same plan as we had in 2002, when he could not finish Kentucky but did well at Bramham.

It seemed like a great idea. Indeed, we were having a good trip at Bramham, with Scotty going like the cross-country machine he was, when disaster struck 200 yards before the last fence. He fell to the ground, dead, having suffered a complete rupture of the aorta. It was the one battle this brave horse couldn't fight back from.

Of course, we'd had no inkling that he had any heart trouble. All too often, such weaknesses don't materialize until you're in the midst of com-petition, when they manifest themselves in an instant—and then it's too late, because they're fatal.

I braced myself to ring Carolyn Todd and tell her the awful news. Scotty died on a Saturday afternoon, which was the middle of the night in New Zealand because of the time difference, so I thought I'd wait until it was morning Down Under to phone Carolyn. The sad thing about my phone call was that someone had beat me to it, a "buddy" who couldn't wait to give her the news.

Carolyn was ever so gracious when I finally got her on the line. Her comment was that she always completely trusted me with Scotty, and that meant a lot.

Regal Scot's death affected a lot of people beyond Carolyn, Mark, David and myself, and Jacquie and the Thompsons. When we phoned home with the news, Sue and all the staff at Stonehall Farm wept terribly. They had nursed Scotty back to health while I was away at both Sydney and Jerez. The whole team was deeply saddened. It even ended the grooming career of Vicky Jessup, who had worked for me for several years. She adored Scotty, who was a very special, loving horse. Everything she had been through with him prompted her to go into another line of work. Scotty probably was one of the smartest horses I've ever ridden. He was a great horse; he just never quite got in the record books.

Mr. Maxwell's passing was the first time I was completely responsible for the death of a horse; it was like having a car wreck when you're the driver and your friend dies in the back seat. With Kilgrogan, I'd had to make a decision as to when he should be put down, with a little window of time for leeway. And with Scotty, there was no decision at all, and no blame. It was just the moment that his stay here on earth was destined to be over.

When bad things happen, it's a time to reflect and learn from your mistakes and the cards fate has dealt you. In the end, you'll find you learn more during the down times than you do during the up times.

And 2002 offered a lot more unhappy opportunities to learn. I had six falls, one of which was fatal to my horse, Louisiana Purchase. This promising young horse, owned by Claude Schock, was running in an Intermediate horse trials when I missed my distance. I came on too long a stride to a table obstacle; he left early and didn't quite clear the jump, smashing down on the top of it.

Although I felt terribly guilty, just as I had about Mr. Maxwell, I somehow was able to have a healthier and less destructive perspective about this tragedy. So I got on and rode my next horse that day, as a statement to other riders that it's important to keep competing. David and I have to think even more carefully now about what we do, because we've become role models, and this was the flip side of that: I certainly didn't want to run that course again that day, but it needed to be done.

Thinking about that awful year, I just gritted my teeth and said, "You've just got to get over yourself and go on." And then I analyzed the situation. I told myself, "OK, six falls are too many. There's got to be something I'm doing wrong."

A lot of what I was trying to do in 2002 was go faster cross-country, and Mark Phillips wanted me to work on balancing the horse without slowing him down. That's been a long project for me, which I'm now starting to understand, both at the horse-trials level and the three-day level. David and I also have the disadvantage of constant pressure; not only the pressure to stay at the top level and make teams, but also the pressure that comes from the position we've put ourselves in by assuming leadership and winding up as role models. And on reflection, I think that one big part of my 2002 problems stemmed from the fact that I was bringing along a new group of horses—who, happily, came into their own in 2003. As always in eventing, if you keep going and have the basic techniques, things can turn around for you.

In 2002, David had come back from getting a team gold medal at the World Equestrian Games to be first at Fair Hill with Custom Made. It was a special event, because (as he's told you) it was Tailor's last three-day, and David really wanted him to go out victorious. It was a heartfelt wish, and when they finished stadium jumping he leaned over in sheer joy and relief to give Tailor a big hug around the neck. An era had ended.

By the next fall, our positions were reversed. I've already mentioned that David wound up in the hospital after his fall with Dunston Celtic on cross-country at Fair Hill 2003, at the same time that things were going great for me: I won the three-star that was being run there along with the Pan Am Championships, thanks to a great effort from

Grand Slam, who's owned by my good friend Lourdes Peralta, best known as Ye Ye.

Of course, I was terribly concerned about David's fall, and the organizing committee was unbelievably sensitive to the fact that I was worried about him *and* trying to compete. While I was in the ten-minute box, they patched him in to me on my cell phone; I spoke to him while he was on the ground. Just moments later, I set off on what was to be one of only seven clean rounds within the optimum time.

The Fair Hill organizers' efforts gave me some reassurance before starting on course. They went out of their way, and I really appreciated it. I think that typifies our whole sport, and how caring we've become as individuals, because we're all in this together and everybody wants everyone to have good, safe rides.

When I show-jumped the next day, David was in an operating room a half-hour's drive away. I thought about him a lot while he was in surgery. We put in a clean round, Grand Slam's best three-star show-jumping performance ever. (After the chaos of the day before, I appreciated a chance to be alone in the arena with my horse. It was so *peaceful* in there!)

I had to ride again in the afternoon for the Pan Am Championships individual-medal race. David had been leading, but the fact that he was in the hospital put Darren Chiacchia—who, like me, was riding as an individual—in first place, riding Windfall, with Will Faudree, a US team member, second. I was third on the Thompsons' horse, Joker's Wild.

Darren was perfect, but Will had some problems that dropped him out of the top three and elevated me to the silver. It was exciting: my first individual medal and, I hoped, a portent of more to come. The clouds had lifted—for me, anyway.

Putting Safety First

There has been a lot of controversy over the quick rise of what was once called the "short format" event and then the CCI without steeplechase. Basically, this concept—used for the 2004 Olympic—drops the steeplechase and the type of roads and tracks that have been key elements in what used to be called the "speed and endurance" phase of a three-day event, a segment that most prominently includes the cross-country test.

The changes have engendered endless hours of discussion and some passionate arguments on both sides. The modification was really pushed by the FEI, and Karen and I don't necessarily agree with how it was fast-tracked, though the motivating factor was keeping eventing in the Olympics. But we'll bet that in five years, the lack of a steeplechase and roads and tracks won't even be noticed.

Anything that contributes to the safety aspect is helpful. The jury is out on the new format, but I don't believe it will improve the safety record of eventing. That depends on the education of horse and rider. We do believe, though, that the sport has gotten safer in its construction and concepts in recent years. However, the problem in this era is that many people are not as educated about riding as they once were in this discipline.

In the old days, competitors came to eventing with a background in different sports, whether it was racing, jumping, hunting or all three, and it just turned out that eventing ended up being their deal.

That is not the case today. People start their competitive careers in eventing and don't have the ability to go out and do all the other things because the countryside has shrunk dramatically. They live in suburbia and board their horses, which means they don't have the access to wide open spaces and a variety of different sports run at speed. That's just a fact of life in the twenty-first century.

So in eventing, our education process has to be expanded to try to help people improve their technique to make them safer. *(continued)*

Don't forget that eventing developed from a cavalry test, which was geared to wartime, where horses and riders were considered expendable. This is completely unacceptable in the modern world.

In recent years, the sport of eventing has taken on board a much more aggressive response to safety of horse and rider from many different directions. Course design and building are so much safer than they used to be. Horses in the previous generation had to jump more out of a single speed. Under the old rules, you could only have two combinations in a course. Now we have to jump many more combinations, and at a variety of speeds, from very slow to very fast. That means the horses have to be much more adjustable and accurate than they were previously. Now there's always some form of a ground line in front of jumps and the fences are fairly ascending, as opposed to square and more difficult to judge.

Communication and ridability are tested more in this era, however, so at times ridability can be more important than ability. Ultimately, education of horse and rider is a much bigger factor. That's why often riders who win are older. When I won the gold medal in Sydney, I was the youngest rider on the podium at age 38.

Meanwhile, instruction of event riders in general is better than it was 25 or 30 years ago, but with that, there are more people doing it, so there are more people hanging out their shingle to teach people.

The US Eventing Association is going after that with the instructor certification program to try to have one recognizable standard of instruction for every level. We're not at the point that you can't teach if you're not certified, but where we'll be 20 years from now, who knows? It will take a lot of time to be able to get the certification program to the point where we're teaching people how to teach, prior to having them give their first lesson. Now we're certifying people who are already there.

CHAPTER NINETEEN

Sharing a laugh with Mark Todd

The People We've Met

WE'VE MADE LOTS of friends worldwide doing the traveling we've done—and, of course, living in England, because that's such an international stage for eventing. We've enjoyed some wonderful times with those friends, outside of the arena as well as in it.

Throughout this book, we've given you brief introductions to eventing's cast of characters, but in this chapter we'll offer a few more impressions about some of the memorable people who have come our way on the circuit, and why they've made such an impact on our lives.

Blyth Tait: During the height of his career, this Olympic and world champion from New Zealand was always the fastest cross-country rider and by far the most competitive person we ever met. He actually raised the bar on competitiveness to new heights. When Karen was winning at

Kentucky on Prince Panache, he clocked her cross-country time with a stopwatch. Blyth, who took pains to be at both the start and finish lines, wanted to make sure her time was correct, and not just take it for granted that the American timers were going to get it right.

Mark Todd: The two-time Olympic individual gold medalist from New Zealand is simply a remarkable rider. The most incredible feat of horsemanship we remember from Mark was the day he broke a stirrup strap early on the cross-country course at Badminton and just kept going to finish clear within the time. This is the toughest course in the world, and he did it with one stirrup. He'd always been at the height of our expectations as a horseman, but that Badminton trip put him into the level of "immortal." *We* couldn't have done that.

Ian Stark: This Scotsman was always the person we liked to watch the most on cross-country. We learned a lot from seeing him go. He had a fearless way of approaching the fences, and he always rode behind the motion to let the horses work. He handled some of the most difficult horses bravely, and he expected his mounts to be incredibly brave. At Gatcombe one year, a stiff test involved jumping up a step and bouncing over a narrow panel. Glenburnie ran out with him—and Ian's disgusted comment as the horse did that was "you bloody chicken!"

Andrew Nicholson: Another New Zealander, another great cross-country rider. You can learn a lot from seeing him go. He's by far the most athletic cross-country rider out there and seriously competitive in that way. When you're around that level of competition, it ends up making *you* better. (That's why we lived in England for as long as we did, and it changed our careers.)

Phillip Dutton: This Australian, based in Pennsylvania, is our Andrew Nicholson here in the US. He's brought a level of competition to this country, at the horse-trials levels, that hasn't been seen here before. He's a very smart guy who learns a lot from situations around him. He's the only person we know besides ourselves who really gets the whole sponsor/public thing—who understands about putting a "team" together.

Mary King: We closely followed this British horsewoman when she made her big decision to start a family. Men on the eventing circuit always used to say that once a woman had her family, she was finished as a competitor. But not Mary. We've admired how competitive she's been about her career, children or no children. In the early '90s, Mary was the one to beat in the world. She is a beautiful cross-country rider—very smooth, very even. She's a sportswoman who always has a smile, but she also has a backbone of steel. She'd run you over with that smile on her face if you got in her way—but you'd still like her while she was doing it.

Bruce Davidson: He's a legend, a two-time world champion who is as tough as nails. Bruce is the comeback kid: Every time you think he's about to retire or he has little in the way of horse quality, he jumps up and does another amazing act. Bruce lives for sport with horses. That's what drives him. He also loves the fact that he has bred champions—and not just horses, but also his own son, Buck. When Bruce dropped rails at Rolex Kentucky in 2003 and ended up down in the order of finish, we couldn't believe how proud he was that Buck became the national spring champion. (That's not to say that at some level he doesn't mind being beaten by his own son, of course.)

Mike Plumb: David's hero when he was a kid. It was an honor for him to ride on the same team with Mike in the 1990 World Championships. This eight-time Olympian is a competitor through and through. Riding and competing were the things he knew how to do best. He may not have been the greatest when it came to people skills—but when he was on a team, he was going to give everything he had and leave it on the playing field; there was no question. He compiled an amazing record.

Tad Coffin: It's a tragedy for the eventing community that Tad, who had so much talent and so much to offer, chose another life after winning two gold medals in the 1976 Olympics. It wasn't the wrong choice, because he enjoys what he does, but the eventing community is the poorer for it.

David Foster: This Irishman was one of the best sportsmen and horsemen we'll ever know. A three-time Olympian, he was killed in an event in April 1998, when his horse flipped and fell on him. He was one of the most popular event riders in the world. His death weighed very heavily on all the top people in the sport at that time. David was such an ambassador for the sport, and such a gentleman. He left behind a lovely wife and two beautiful kids. It was so senseless that he died competing at Preliminary level on a young horse, going over a very innocuous jump into water—and something that made us all realize that you can get injured at any level. There were thousands of people from all over the world at his funeral, mourning a man who still had the best of his career and life with his family to come.

©BRANT GAMMA

Together, ready for anything that comes our way

The Next Chapter

DAVID: No matter how well you prepare and bring along your horses, there's no insurance against disaster. I think you make your own good luck through hard work, persistence, and optimism. But you also need an absence of bad luck, like not having a horse step on a stone the day before the Olympic Games.

That realization really struck me after Giltedge and Custom Made retired. I was looking toward the 2004 Olympics and had gotten a horse, Shiraz, who actually may have been the most talented animal that I ever rode. When we bought him, I thought everything seemed to be arranged for that moment. Going down to New Zealand, seeing him, liking him, riding him, and having him come back and be more of a horse than I thought he was got me excited. He was the horse I was looking for, and I thought, "The whole thing has been set up to come to this point."

Chapter 20 | *The Next Chapter*

I got Raz in the summer of 2003—and as I trained him, the Athens Olympics seemed like a real possibility for him. But three and a half months later he was dead, so badly injured in a freak pasture accident that he couldn't be saved. That was the start of a run of seriously bad luck that tested my commitment.

A few weeks later, I was riding Dunston Celtic at Fair Hill in the open three-star division, being held there in tandem with the Pan American Championships. Earlier in the day, I'd moved into the lead in the Pan Am standings with Courting Danger—and felt as if I could practically touch the individual Pan Am gold medal that had eluded me in 1999. Then, halfway around the course on Dunston Celtic, I saw a distance that was too long to a fence. He took off but didn't make it, and we both crashed to the ground. My left ankle and wrist were broken. Forget the Pan Ams; I was taken to the hospital immediately. At the time that I should have been finishing the show-jumping course the next day, I was just coming out of anesthesia from a lengthy operation.

Was this a sign that I wasn't meant to go to the 2004 Olympics? When Raz died, I'd been shaken, very affected by his loss. The whole game changed for me. I had already put myself in a frame of mind where the Athens Olympics were less important to me than the Sydney Games. If I went, I told myself, I'd try just as hard as I always did—but I knew that if I didn't get there, it wouldn't devastate me.

I decided that 2004 would be my last try for a championships team, Olympic or otherwise. As I've mentioned previously, when you ride on a team—as opposed to riding for yourself—you have a lot more hoops to jump through. You also have a lot more responsibilities: to your country and your teammates as well as to your horse, his owner, and yourself.

I am very proud of the ways I have been able to help our team effort, but now it's time to let other riders carry that torch. At the same time, I'm always available to give advice and do what I can, whether as president of our Federation or as a coach, to make sure our flag flies high at major international events.

Ian Stark, the Scottish rider I have long admired, has done just what I'm doing. He bowed out of the team fray but has continued competing as an individual at major events. That keeps him a presence in the sport while lessening the demands that start to be more of a burden as we age. So riding and competing will still be a big part of my life, even without the team commitment.

I'm excited about working with younger horses for the sake of training and competing. I have no idea whether I'll sell them or compete them myself. I'm very much back to training, riding, and competing for the joy of doing it, and not just a specific goal. When you ride at the top level for so long, that goal becomes the only test of success—but that's where I think I've changed. It can't be the only reason you're still doing this.

I get a real big kick out of the training part, and I enjoy the everyday events. When you determine your success only by whether you make the Olympic team, that's going to be unhealthy for the long term, because you have to have something else.

I've been at the top of the game for a long time. In the early years, I was always striving, wondering if I was good enough. Yet I've always played down the big wins—if you put them too high, the lows are too low.

By this time, I've pretty much fulfilled all my riding ambitions. The one thing I've missed doing is getting a team gold medal in the Olympics, something that (as of this writing) hasn't happened for a US eventing team since 1984. I would like to be a part of that; feeling I could contribute something is more important to me than another individual gold. That's because the team thing always has meant more to me than the individual.

I believe in taking the horses you have and doing the best you can with them, but it's always harder when you don't have the talent in your string that you once enjoyed. As Karen puts it, "There's nothing like a good horse to make everyone think you're riding great." My frustration in

2003 and going into 2004 was about not doing a good enough job and not having the horses to play the game the way I wanted to.

Just as Karen and I have different strengths in the way we run our lives, we also have different strengths when it comes to horses. I don't think I'm as good as Karen is at coaching an individual rider. But I've been named the US Olympic Committee's equestrian Developmental Coach of the Year for my work with young riders to prepare them for team situations. And I'm very good at training horses, as well as talking about training horses. So I have lots of possibilities out there for the time when I'm not competing at championship level anymore.

Whatever we do, Karen and I both believe in giving back to the sport. We would like to train horses that go up to the top level, and we're now blessed with the most talented students we've ever had. Is the next group of students going to be as talented as this one? Who knows? You just go on teaching and see what happens.

The Olympic Games, a focal point of our lives for so long, are about the process of doing things in an excellent way, and that's taught us a lot. You need to take that process and apply it to your next goal, whatever it is, whether it's coaching students or coaching a team, designing courses or managing an event or a federation.

I don't think we're any better than the riders or teachers who came before us or will come after us. But we have a different approach that's given us opportunities. We enjoy going in front of 10,000 people and telling them about horses and training in a way that they can understand, have a laugh, and be entertained. It's all about promoting horse sports. (Notice that I said "horse sports," not just "eventing.")

Our sport, at the moment, is totally client-based. That means you, your horse's owner, or your family pays for it. We'd like to see that change. Other sports are spectator- and public-based. Before we can bring in the public, attract spectators who'll be interested in our sport, we have to look at ourselves. Are we entertaining? If not, why not?

It's not about changing what we do. It's about showmanship.

When surveys show that every third family in America wants something to do with horses, you're dealing with a lot of possibilities for marketability. What makes it tough for marketing the horse industry is the fact that we're so fragmented. I don't see us having anything to sell to the masses until we unify as an industry and stop being so territorial about our segments of it. A horse is a horse; they all process information the same way.

As Karen and I continue our careers and lives, we've never ever thought about doing something outside the horse world. There's too much to do *in* the horse world that can keep you occupied, interested and stimulated. If you're stimulated, you're still pushing the boundaries and trying to get better, just as you did when you were riding.

What have we learned from horses? So many, many things—including things you can translate to human interaction. Among them are patience and communication, and knowing how to make things the other person's idea. We've also learned, the hard way, that you can't win all the time. That's life, not just horses.

David J. O'Connor

KAREN: The silver medal that I earned with Joker's Wild at the 2003 Pan American Championships was the first individual medal I ever won. There's still a big part of me that would like to win another individual medal against the best in the world on a particular day, at the Olympics or the World Championships.

Hitting my mid-40s, I'm proud to say my riding is improving, and I want to keep going. Why do I have the hunger and the competitive spirit to continue longer? Because I feel as if I'm only just getting it sorted out in my head.

There were parts of my career that I struggled through, for a variety of reasons. I struggled with the dressage at the beginning of my career because I didn't have a strong dressage background. I struggled in the middle part of my career to be faster on cross-country because I was riding horses that were too big for me. I didn't understand how to ride a big horse fast.

On the other hand, show jumping is something I've always been stronger at because I had a background in that, from training with Colonel John Russell and Julie Ulrich. I've learned more about show jumping through the programs at the USET, working with George Morris and Anne Kursinski and the other great jumper riders who have provided us with instruction.

So putting that all together, I have a big hankering to keep going. How long will I go? I say to my fellow competitors, "If I start riding really badly, will you guys put me out of my misery?" If I keep going and David doesn't, I know he'll be supportive, but it will change the dynamics of our relationship—because we will have to make an effort we've never had to make before, that would be much more like the effort of the normal married couple: learning how to balance our time away and our time together. If he's off doing committee or coaching work and I'm off competing, we'll have to make it work logistically.

And we will make it work, because at the end of the day, there isn't anything more important to us than our marriage. However things play out in the next few years, it will be a new challenge, and we'll work through it.

Even after I do my last international competition, I'll still have a depth of education that is a conglomeration of a lot of other people's effort that I won't let go to waste. You put thirty or thirty-five years of your life into one thing and there's knowledge there, knowledge that you've gleaned through experience, through other people's teaching, and through your horses. I would like to think that by sharing that knowledge I would benefit other people and other horses more than I'm able to do now because

I devote so many hours to competing myself, with all that involves.

I love to train horses that are confused, to give them confidence in their own lives to do whatever the task is; and I love to instruct. These last couple of years that I'm competing, it's kind of like my special time. Luckily, I have good students who understand and respect that. David and I are careful about the time we spend with our own horses now. As you get older, you need to work more at being fit; your technique is good, but you need to practice the application of your technique so you don't lose your edge.

One thing I know for sure: Even after I finish competing, animals will always be key in whatever I do. For me, there is no question that life with animals definitely completes me, because my life has always had to have animals. More specifically the horses have taught me, as the dogs have taught me, that they are innocent and domesticated, but not by choice. That gives you a daunting responsibility to do the right thing. If you take on board that responsibility, to do the right thing, it's a rule to live by.

Horses are comfort animals. They like to do good things to make their herd feel better about them. If you're their leader, they want to please you. That means you have a responsibility to them, and it's one we have always taken seriously.

We hope you've enjoyed sharing the story of our journey. Perhaps it will inspire you to work harder with your riding, or look at it from a different angle. We wish you the best of luck on your journey with horses—may it be a long and happy one, as ours has been. And maybe we'll meet you along the way.

Karen O'Connor

The Plains, Virginia
June 2004

David O'Connor (Through June 2004)

• INTERNATIONAL COMPETITION RESULTS •

Year	Placing	Event
2004	1st	Foxhall CCI*** (Outlawed)
2003	15th	Burghley CCI**** GBR (Tigger Too)
2003	1st	Jersey Fresh CCI** (Gorta Glen)
2003	8th	Bramham CCI*** GBR (Courting Danger)
2002	1st	Fair Hill CCI*** MD (Custom Made)
2002	Team Gold	World Equestrian Games, Jerez, SPA (Giltedge)
2001	1st	Fair Hill CCI*** MD (The Native)
2001	2nd	Radnor CCI** PA (Persistant Rain)
2001	1st	Rolex Kentucky CCI**** (Giltedge)
2000	Team Bronze	Olympic Games, Sydney, AUS (Giltedge)
2000	Individual Gold	Olympic Games, Sydney, AUS (Custom Made)
2000	8th	Foxhall CCI*** GA (Giltedge)
2000	2nd	Rolex Kentucky CCI**** (Rattle 'N' Hum)
1999	1st	Fair Hill CCI*** MD (Rattle 'N' Hum)
1999	4th	Blenheim CCI*** GBR (Custom Made)
1999	Team Gold	Pan American Games, Winnipeg, CAN (Giltedge)
1999	Individual Silver	Pan American Games, Winnipeg, CAN (Giltedge)
1999	1st	North American Beaulieu CIC*** GA (Giltedge)
1998	Team Bronze	World Equestrian Games, Rome, ITA (Giltedge)
1998	6th	World Equestrian Games, Rome, ITA (Giltedge)
1997	1st	Fair Hill CCI*** MD (Giltedge)
1997	2nd	Fair Hill CCI*** MD (Lightfoot)
1997	3rd	Punchestown CCI*** IRE (Giltedge)
1997	1st	Badminton CCI**** GBR (Custom Made)
1996	Team Silver	Olympic Games, Atlanta, GA (Giltedge)
1996	5th Individual	Olympic Games, Atlanta, GA (Custom Made)
1995	1st	Fair Hill CCI*** MD (Giltedge)
1995	1st	Rolex Kentucky CCI*** (Custom Made)
1994	43rd	Individual and Team Alternate, World Equestrian Games, The Hague, NED (On A Mission)
1993	1st	Fair Hill CCI*** MD (Wilton Fair)
1993	1st	Gatcombe Park Horse Trials GBR (Lighter Than Air)
1992	7th	Badminton CCI**** GBR (Wilton Fair)

(continued)

1990	1st	Rolex Kentucky CCI*** (Wilton Fair)
1988		Alternate, Olympic Games, Seoul, KOR (Take The Rapids)
1986	2nd	Individual and Team Alternate, World Championship CCI*** Bialy Bor, POL (Border Raider)

• AWARDS •

2002 USA Equestrian Horseman of the Year

2001 USA Equestrian Horseman of the Year

1999 USCTA Horse of the Year (Rattle 'N' Hum)

1999 USCTA Leading Rider (Also received in 1998, 1997, 1996)

1998 Whitney Stone Cup

1997 USCTA Horse of the Year (Lightfoot)

1997 AHSA Zone 3 Champion Combined Training, Advanced Level (Giltedge)

1997 USOC Olympic Athlete of the Month (May)

1997 USET Rider of the Month (May)

1997 USOC "Male Equestrian Athlete of the Year"

1997 Virginia Horse Council Rider of the Year (David and Karen O'Connor)

1996 USCTA Horse of the Year (Custom Made)

• RIDER RANKING •

	FEI	National
2003	—	10th
2002	19th	4th
2001	1st	3rd
2000	1st	3rd
1999	5th	1st
1998	6th	3rd
1997	3rd	1st

Karen O'Connor (Through June 2004)

• INTERNATIONAL COMPETITION RESULTS •

Year	Placing	Event
2003	Individual Silver	Pan American Games CCI*** Fair Hill, MD (Joker's Wild)
2003	1st	Fair Hill CCI*** MD (Grand Slam)
2003	5th	Blenheim CCI*** GBR (Bally Mar)
2003	6th	Rolex Kentucky CCI**** (Upstage)
2003	7th	Rolex Kentucky CCI**** (Joker's Wild)
2003	15th	Foxhall CCI*** GA (Bally Mar)
2002	8th	Blenheim CCI*** GBR (Joker's Wild)
2002	13th	Bramham CCI*** GBR (Regal Scot)
2002	10th	Foxhall CCI*** GA (Travis)
2002	12th	Rolex Kentucky CCI**** (Grand Slam)
2001	5th	Fair Hill CCI*** MD (Upstage)
2001	6th	Radnor CCI** PA (Beringer)
2001	1st	Foxhall CCI*** GA (Prince Panache)
2000	6th	Radnor CCI** PA (Upstage)
2000	Team Bronze	Olympic Games, Sydney, AUS (Prince Panache)
2000	3rd	Bromont CCI** CAN (Travis)
2000	3rd	Rolex Kentucky CCI**** (Prince Panache)
1999	2nd	Fair Hill CCI*** MD (Regal Scott)
1999	1st	Rolex Kentucky CCI**** (Prince Panache)
1998	Team Bronze	World Equestrian Games, Rome, ITA (Prince Panache)
1998	5th	Badminton CCI**** GBR (Prince Panache)
1998	5th	Rolex Kentucky CCI**** (Biko)
1997	Team Member	European Championship CCI*** GBR (Prince Panache)
1997	1st	Rolex Kentucky CCI*** (Worth the Trust)
1996	3rd	Fair Hill CCI*** MD (Worth The Trust)
1996	Team Silver	Olympic Games, Atlanta, GA (Biko)
1995	8th	European Open Championship CCI*** ITA (Biko)
1995	3rd	Checkmate CCI** CAN (Worth The Trust)
1995	3rd	Badminton CCI**** GBR (Biko)
1994	5th	Burghley CCI**** GBR (Prince Panache)
1994	11th	World Equestrian Games, The Hague, NED (Biko)
1993	5th	Fair Hill CCI*** MD (Prince Panache)
1993	6th	Blenheim CCI*** GBR (Biko)

(continued)

1993	1st	Punchestown CCI*** IRE (Shannon)
1993	3rd	Punchestown CCI*** IRE (Enniskerry)
1992	3rd	Loughanmore CCI** IRE (Biko)
1991	3rd	Burghley CCI*** GBR (Mr. Maxwell)
1991	1st	Rolex Kentucky CCI*** (Mr. Maxwell)
1989	1st	Fair Hill CCI*** MD (Nos Ecus)
1988	Team Member	Olympic Games, Seoul, KOR (The Optimist)
1986	4th	Alternate World Championship CCI*** Bialy Bor, POL (The Optimist)
1986	18th	World Championships CCI**** Gawler, AUS (Lutin V)
1985	1st	Fall Championship, Chesterland, PA (Castlewellan)
1984	1st	Boekelo, CCI*** NED (The Optimist)

• AWARDS •

2003 USCTA Lady Rider of the Year (Also received in 2000, 1998, 1997, 1996, 1995, 1991, 1990, 1989)

2000 Whitney Stone Cup

2000 Armada Cup, Badminton, completed 5 times

2000 USCTA Horse of the Year (Prince Panache)

1999 USCTA Horse of the Century (Biko)

1993 US Olympic Committee Female Equestrian Athlete of the Year

1993 3rd place World Three-Day Event Rider Rankings, L'Annee Hippique

1991 6th place World Three-Day Event Rider Rankings, L'Annee Hippique

• RIDER RANKING •

	FEI	National
2003	5th	3rd
2002	28th	3rd
2001	9th	5th
2000	7th	4th
1999	8th	7th
1998	14th	3rd
1997	7th	4th